NEW
AMERICAN
POETRY

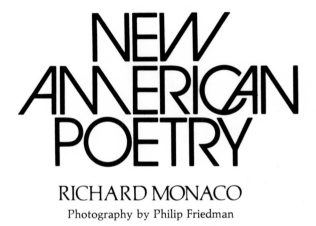

NEW AMERICAN POETRY

RICHARD MONACO

Photography by Philip Friedman

McGRAW-HILL BOOK COMPANY

New York   St. Louis   San Francisco   Düsseldorf   Johannesburg
Kuala Lumpur   London   Mexico   Montreal   New Delhi
Panama   Rio de Janeiro   Singapore   Sydney   Toronto

NEW AMERICAN POETRY

123456789HDMB798765432

This book was set in Patina by University Graphics, Inc. The editors were David Edwards and James R. Belser; the designer was Rafael Hernandez; and the production supervisor was Sally Ellyson.
The printer was Halliday Lithograph Corporation; the binder, The Maple Press Company.

Library of Congress Cataloging in Publication Data

Monaco, Richard.
    New American poetry.

    1. American poetry—20th century. I. Title
PS615.M55   811'.5'408   72-6571
ISBN 0-07-042678-3

ACKNOWLEDGMENTS

Photography by Philip Friedman (pp. 2, 12, 18, 74, 96, 126, 136, 190), John Briggs (pp. x, 56, 64, 88, 160, 174, 184), Hilary (p. 46), John Payne (p. 28), Tom Peck (p. 110), and William Stafford (p. 82).
    The cover sculpture by Ulrich Niemeyer was photographed by Bob Weir.

John Briggs: "A Beach for Martin Heidegger," *New York Quarterly.*

Christopher Collins: "Catullus among the Tiger Lilies," *New York Poetry.*

David Galler: "The Stonecutter's Resignation," *Hudson Review;* "Hope," *The Nation;* "The Mountaineers," *Poetry Northwest.*

Dick Gallup: "Bird Life," *The New York Times;* "Call It Egypt" and "Like the Stars," *The World Magazine;* "Relaxation," *An Anthology of New York Poets,* published by Random House; "Living Together," "Bird Life," "Call It Egypt," "Where I Hang My Hat," "Like the Stars," "Relaxation" from *Where I Hang My Hat* by Dick Gallup. Copyright © 1970 by Dick Gallup; reprinted by permission of Harper & Row, Publishers, Inc.

Philip Levine: "Thistles," "¡Hola Miguelin!" and "Autumn," *Hudson Review;* "How Much Can It Hurt?" *Kayak;* "Robert," *New American Review.*

Louis Phillips: "Rus in Urbe," *New York Poetry;* "A Metaphor Carried Almost to Excess," "Sequence for My Lady," "Love & the Telephone Company," and "78 Miners in Mannington, West Virginia," *Prologue Magazine.*

David Posner: "Dialogue with the Countess," *New York Poetry.*

Dwight Robhs: "Crazed by Earthlight" and "Little Egypt," *Prologue Magazine.*

Karen Swenson: "Why Didn't Anyone Tell Hester Prynne?" *Beloit Poetry Journal;* "Dear Elizabeth," *Prairie Schooner;* "A Family," *Denver Quarterly.*

Jean Valentine: "Solomon," *Commonweal;* "The Summer House," *Poetry;* "In the Museum," *Radcliffe Poetry;* "Solomon," "The Summer House," and "In the Museum" reprinted with the permission of Farrar, Straus & Giroux, Inc. from *Pilgrims* by Jean Valentine, copyright © 1965, 1966, 1969 by Jean Valentine.

Douglas Worth: "Cocoons at the Window," *Colorado Quarterly;* "Married 2½ Weeks," "Strap Hanger," "Muse," and "Metamorphoses," *Prologue Magazine;* "The Return," *New York Poetry.*

CONTENTS

INTRODUCTION

Poets have a way of getting lost fast or of never getting found in the first place. Young or old, they ride the same fame-waves that lift and drop politicians and movie stars, except that while the peaks are considerably less high, the troughs are deeper. Fame is good for the ego, but since it doesn't do much for the rest of a person, perhaps keeping power and glory away from a poet is like disarming a murderous man: it leaves the urge to kill but restricts the means.

Movie stars depend on the circumstances of film production and no one thinks much of a politician unless he's holding some post or other, but a poet can be a poet whenever he's able. He doesn't need the machinery of the world to provide the means for him. When you are lucky enough to be able to devote less of yourself to the world than most people, then you have to expect to get less of it in return.

The only real reward a poet can hope for, most of the time, is in doing the best possible job on each poem, since it may never be read anyway. But, looking at life honestly, the only permanent possessions people have are love and wisdom—if in fact they aren't the same thing—and after sorting out the complex appearances of poetic language and systems, it turns out that the object of experiencing poetry is to make discoveries—whether about the poet, the art, or the world—in the fervent hope of wisdom. When a writer turns out to be silly, very limited, or trivial (very often even if there's no big question of talent), it's frequently because he is unable to free himself from desires and pretensions long enough to learn anything. You might almost say the best poet is the one who can forget his art and his opinions while in the process of writing. And that, as all sages agree, is the only road to wisdom. Playing with words is its own reward. Take away a rich man's money and he's a poor man; denude a wise one and nothing's changed much.

Obviously everyone in this collection is not a poetic sage, and some may never come close, but the idea here is to resist, as best we can, the normal tendency to publish either without sufficient discrimination or with far too much. An editor's limits can get narrowed by what he knows best and feels most comfortable with. Of course he can't do much with things that baffle him completely. A position somewhere in the middle is necessary, and we've tried to strike it.

Readers are affected, understandably, by what gets most promoted. If enough editors publish this school or that person, the audience, in time, gets the impression that the best known must be best, and it's a hard illusion to dispel. Fame ought to be considered a failure of spiritual ecology.

The people in this collection vary in age from about twenty-two to about fifty. Some are more developed in their art than others, some have more sociological interest than art.

Objectively, poets since Edenic days have had much in common. A real definition of poetry results from observation of the practice of centuries. Poets learn from masters and the masters have much in common, so a continuity remains. In English poetry over the past five centuries very little has changed other than point of view: people still write sonnets and sestinas (now and then) and worry about love and death, war and God, etc., etc. How writers move with a tradition or counter it or just play around the outskirts certainly is not as important as the depth, impact, and beauty of their works, but it's pointless to talk about why one man is deeper than another. Discovering that is a measure of one's own depth. It is easier to notice the peculiarities of a writer's manner.

Now, an extreme case of countering tradition can be seen in Clark Coolidge's work. If you look back over the past five centuries, you won't find poems very much like his. By the definition suggested above you might even say he isn't actually writing poetry at all. Perhaps not, but he is undeniably dealing with some of its basic elements, and in a way he's writing *about* poems: his work sets up a condition, a word climate, where meaning is obliquely suggested, not actually established, and an abstract sound pattern is evoked. In most poetry these dimensions are manifested in a secondary role (even in Cummings, for example), and the flow of overall meaning is primary. Coolidge uses these secondary elements as the subject matter of each piece. This might be said to place him on the extreme left of the collection. Richard Kostelanetz inhabits the same neighborhood, but in his case the work keys off the fact that poetry is generally printed on a page. His words and letters are patterned into abstractions with minimal non-visual content.

Over to the right of center we find poets such as David Galler, Christopher Collins, Richard Hugo, John Briggs, and Dwight Robhs. In these writers techniques common to every poetic age can be distinguished quite clearly—not to say that these characteristics are absent from the bulk of the poets comprising the center, just that among the poets on the right they are particularly easy to see. A continuity of tradition has been maintained on nearly every level.

In the center, Philip Levine, Karen Swenson, Gary Livingston, and Dick Gallup, for example, treat aspects of metaphoric formality and continuity quite freely. In general, their diction and manner are less formal than that of the more traditional poets.

These distinctions are intended only as a rough-and-ready means of pointing out superficial characteristics and have nothing to do with so-called schools of writing. What mainly set poets apart from one another are matters of personality and talent. Variance in technique has little to do with the level of ability or achievement.

The poets in this book cover a respectably comprehensive range in everything from manner to subject matter, youth to middle age, urban to pastoral, avant-garde to conservative. Our purpose has been not so much to enshrine every line between these covers as it has been to try to freeze an image of poetry as a living, growing art in contemporary America. The poets here who have (as they used to say) struck eternal fire from their verse will enshrine themselves, in any case, past our power.

JOHN BRIGGS *John Briggs, who was born in 1945, lives, studies, and works in New York City. Formerly managing editor of* New York Poetry, *he is at the present time managing editor of* New York Quarterly. *He is a graduate of Wesleyan University, and has been a reporter and a teacher.*

YUKON 1897: PRICE OF GOLD
after Jack London

His breath a blear of warmth across the vast white
stilled unreal snowfields—
through the feral silence—on the webs
of snowshoes, the old prospector shuffles
heading North.
His lean and faithful dog trots on beside him.

The old man dreams of glory-holes of gold—
dreams the sharp cold gaudy heat
of nuggets—drags his aging breath across
these frozen wastes men
civilize by greed—across this blank and zero world
of cold.
He hikes through frozen air
as though through solid ice.

Too late, on ice, he knows of his mistake—
across a buried lake he feels the crack and craze
of webbed uncertainness beneath him—
and sinking through receives a shock
that squeezes out his breath.

Fingers numb, he kneels and prays
for flame (learns, warmth is real
as riches that he'd looked for).
But yellow nugget-bursts of matches break and fly
and sputter out—
his body fading out,
the sharp cold
presses in.

Beneath the frozen sky
the old man sinks into a snowdrift;
in total cold feels somehow warm.
In soft snow dreams gaudily . . .
A spider with a body like a nugget
spins his breath like threads
—his vision blurs

and webs
with longings . . .

In stark cold air, the stark primeval dog
sniffs briefly at the scents of missing life.

TAO SĀSHE: THE TREACHEROUS COURTESAN

"They say the icy dragon wind breathes
fiercely in the savage crags tonight.
You will notice, Precious Sir, how slight the strain
its chill makes on our gentle air."
The youthful swordsman idles in the flawless gardens,
awaiting the appearance of the famous Tao Sāshe.
"I have come from the mountains," he says,
"And there the cruel barbarians strain our gates."
Among compliant shadows, blown (as though a candle)
out, the servant bows.
And in the boughs of tapered willow leaves
the last cool light glows,
frailly white.
The legendary warning is forgotten:
'Beware of the treacherous Tao—
her kiss is slender
and her eyes are wild;
along her clever paths the careless swordsman may mislay
his sword.'

On faultless paths is whispering the delicate Tao.
The evening poised as crystal, the
fountain pools are still, look
touched with chillness in the failing light.
Careful words spoken in the silk-cool air:
"There in the tangled woods,
beyond these formal gardens," she explains,
"roam tigers and the wild bear. Here,
from on our terrace, by the glow of lanterns,
one can see their eyes." Tarnished
silver petals of the moonflowers
gleam, a rill's slim water slips,
in glassy silence, through the rocks:
Careless nature to Tao's artful whim
has been detained . . .

The darkness faded pale by moonlight,
the swordsman lies on cool sheets
in formal fragrance.
The world seems slender as the moon
upon a swordedge
poised.

The warrior feels expectant (who has recalled
her eyes were lowered),
is graciously forgetful . . .
A shadowy branch taps out the wind's
vague message
on a glow of windowscreen.
He shivers here
with ecstacy (or fear),
knows Perfect Tao has come . . .

Thin as a petal he feels her tongue;
as cool as silk or whispering she slips.
The chill reflection arced (it glints),
the wishful swordsman sees
the sliver of his hungry face
loom palely
in the mooncut silver.
The silken hiss he
barely hears . . .

OF MERE BEING

A Variation for Wallace Stevens

In the fog at the end of the mind,
Beyond the last thought,
a gaunt tree rises
(in the pale distance)

The tree is stark,
—and in its branches, black with rain,
appears a bird: a
quick bird,
frail
and not exotic.

The tree stands at the edge of space;
the fog clings palely to its branches.
The body of the bird
flicks,
its head jerks up . . .
The eye is furious.

A BEACH FOR MARTIN HEIDEGGER

The sky and sea are one
in gray. Above
(a fragment
like a thought) a lone gull
drifts
and
falls.
And at the ocean's thinning edge
I stand—
to watch the water's protoplasmic pulse
(like time
this vast amoeba swells and shrinks)
—along an empty coast.
The shard of gull cries once, and then
is gone—
into that gray
its cry
uncannily
defines

LOGIC OF REFLECTION

He discovered something in the strangeness
of his face in a hallway mirror.
He found that the mirror was a door,
and then a corridor,
down which he echoed—
a disreputable hotel.
He was in his own mind.
The corridor was poorly lit,
was cramped,
interminable,
and lined with locked, warped doors
(In endless rooms
sad dreams and terrors.).

Before a door like Memory
he stops and gawks,
like an amnesiac,
before a door he knows
will fly
open to his hand.
And here a dark strange plain
Across it blows a wind
Blows through the mirror—
This cold, black, spatial wind

Abolishes him

LUCID PRODIGY IN SNOW

for Joe LaRocca

The winter buries things.
The world is shapeless in a generality
of snow.
I hike across
a strangely frozen landscape (to feel
alone) . . .
The icebound lake lies absolute
and
still;
air seems airless; far-off trees
look stark . . .

Across the cold and abstract land I tramp
—and find—above a buried stream—
a pool of ice,
where wind has blown
a fragment's clearness . . .
(view another world)

Around me evening settles
dim and cold. Long winds stir.
Flakes across the silent desolation
swirl

and I retreat.
Across the darkened snowland go—and
know a secret fear that bends me homeward:

know the wind that blows such cosmic snow
has blown through all dark space

EDWARD   *Edward Butscher, born in 1938, is a resident of New*
BUTSCHER   *York City, where he writes and teaches. His work*
has been published in a number of poetry magazines and literary
journals. He attended C. W. Post College.

ARCTIC GRACE

I

Like an iceberg, groaning and
growing from its crystal self,
the mind moves slowly into winter.

Innocent of seasons, ghostly herds
of bison congeal their desperate
breath into downy fields,

bellowing water lilies at each
root shot, the first sharp fang,
become a mammoth dancing bear

chained by golden hordes of naked
Indians, mountain and foothills
to the frozen-mad sea.

II

Behind window frosts, arterial
philosophies harden with hoary age
into the arthritic talons

of graveyard spinsters, ripping
aside hard snow to slash at dawn's
grim pregnancies, keening long winds

through black and spindle boughs
like the singing corn silk
of their own floral patterned pasts,

the hunched, erect and flyer
contaminated, so elaborately frail,
by tissue, blood and being.

Like an iceberg, groaning and
growing from its crystal self,
the mind moves slowly into winter.

THE BENCH SAYER

I listen to children
breaking one another,
as they break the hard earth,
and hear her ginghams overhead
rustle into flames
that tear away flesh.

    Autumn comes finally
    with whispers of bronze death,
    athletes wrenching the sun
    from my cloud-muscled heart
    and smashing it against slate fields
    until chestnuts moan, fall.

Sitting alone inside old age,
I wonder if the squirrels
will carry off her bones.

PASSAGE TO MANHATTAN

Sparrows pour through the haze
of bad dreams, seeding
leafless, lifeless roods
atop the drifted tombs
with their own soft selves,
as the dawn's gold yolk
breaks in his glassy hair,

our father who walks
upon concrete seas
for us, for us,

breaking daisy chains
against money-green knees
for us, for us,

before the descent,
devils breaking, too,
beneath his steel toes,

while mists, like myths,
like ragged children
dance, weeping, around
his stalking form, scattered
by his neatness,
his mad eyes.

STILL LIFE

Unaware
of enraged suns
pounding at locked
claws, bats, not
necessarily vampires,
hang like downy
fruit from sea-cold
eaves of a secret
lair, drip, plump
and dusk-gray,
in a content
mass,

unaware, too,
of willows breaking
delicate
toes
against
their slate darkness.

They sleep
without sound
and refuse recognition
to the wind's
sway
until
reversals
turn their planet,

then emerge
as screams
from the slack jaws
of night,
dribbled into flight
by deep repose
and ancient yearnings
for the moon's
pale blood.

CHRISTOPHER Christopher Collins, who was born in 1937,
COLLINS lives in New York City and is an assistant professor
at New York University. He has written theoretical books on poetry—
The Act of Poetry, published by Random House; The Web of
Observation, published by Mouton—and has prepared a translation of
Longus' Daphnis & Chloê for the Imprint Society.

ATLANTIC NIGHT TRIP

FAR

from bingo far from pingpong
far from gingercookies far from deckchairs
far from phrasebook blanket spit spray
and each painful hammered sundown,

far from parties deodorants cheap scotch
hysteria canapes dancing cabins
of joyous rat-eyed virgins dispensing
their last remnants of diddled honor:

Some wired icon waits for me,
too doomed to die, some palaver harp
plucked by her own two chicken hands.
(While the band in the ballroom boomed

the Mexican Hat Dance and the Hora,
"They'll never understand," said she,
clawing the label off the sweaty beer,
"how useless all this really is.")

I search this ship for crippled Diana
through moony phases of cocktail lounges:
long white childish cheeks
and the clank of contraptions underneath,

BUT

there is no moon tonight.

Connect the distances.

The lights of eight ships to the north
one to the west
three each to the south and east
bead the horizon.

Connect the distances.

The future
so soft to the touch   it opens on either side
and closes about us
holding us homeward weaving continuously the threads of our passage

Connect the distances.

The deck slopes
the waters at the stern churn in starshine
the constellations spread like fingers
and give way to this slow irruption into vacant space

Connect the distances.

The voices below deck
lose themselves, return, and are ripped away on the wind
to be webbed upon unimaginable stillness
where not a word a fingertouch a glint in glass is lost
    in this whole lost world

Connect the distances.

We coast over the sleep of Atlantis
and under stars which Atlas hung high up in the branches of the tree
of the night the shepherds spied the daughters of Hesperos
dancing slowly across the sky in the coldness before first light

Connect the distances
connect the distances
connect the distances.

Connect the distances,

AND

Good night
there is nearness here

a sunken harbor
where the old things are

clustered beyond all cycles
heaved only by the deep tides.

What was I thinking of so long so long?
waiting so long for the unreal to surface
while mermen under the sea ruled and watched
wharves cargoed with casks of sweetnesses

reality so long enriching itself in Egyptian darkness
crushed liquors crusting themselves over with iridescence.

Harbored where the Sky Boat rocks at anchor
no thing is lost or alien or very far from

the touch of the lover's hand of the darkness
the hidden the obvious the undeniable

the tender delirium
singing ceaselessly

at the heart
of being

I

am always
an unforeseen event

a deliberate mistake for which
all things are responsible.

Perhaps it is possible to live
without triviality or bitterness

I am not hedged by the lights I see
the stars are cabled to my hands and eyes

my arms begin to ache from the haul of the wind of the world
in my skysails and the deep water sucks at colossal feet.

THE HOMECOMING

The house is gone, torn down, yet I've come back
and walk from room to room and see it all
just as I left it twenty years ago.
There's my father sleeping in his chair
under the feeble light, his newspaper
across his knees. I walk on quietly.
Isn't it strange, I say to myself, he's gone
but somehow remains here. And my mother too,
I see her standing by the kitchen table,
locked in that other time of photographs.

Outside, in a celluloid negative sundown
the lawn slopes westward upward among the trees
where a dirt road continues, then turns somewhere
away.

      It was there in the dimness of that roadside
that, before I reached the dark lawn, I clipped out
a single gentian. See? I have brought it here
and placed it in a clear vase, in my bedroom, on the windowsill.

(I think I hear my parents breathing softly
in another room. Their sleep is good tonight.
I must not stir them in their sleep.)
                      The moon!
Look how it drifts up in the summer dark
of twenty years ago.
             And blue cut gentian,
don't you accuse me of your severed life.
My brother, I am as innocent as you.

It's fun sometimes to stay awake alone.

Hear how my voice echoes through this vacant family.

There's a whole night to watch through till the end.

And there is freedom for us both which—look,
my little flower—full in this dead room
the rip-cloud moon now manifests.

CATULLUS AMONG THE TIGER LILIES

They keep their gardens under strict surveillance,
Those hieroglyphic elders with chased faces
Like friezes graven in Ecbatana—
But we "My Lesbia, let us live, etc."

Look up now: see them in their porticoes? . . .
Clutching their clippers lest the restless flowers,
Subject to bees of indeterminate sex,
Riot and strenuously copulate:

Beneath the radar of their rheumy eyes
We, hiding among the tiger lilies, crouch:
O do not move when I make love to you—
The corrugated elders might grow pale,

And, Lesbia, paler than their trembling staffs
They'd clamber up the iris-violet sky
And lay hands on the carven robes of God
To shake him from the stonework of his sleep.

These scrannel courtiers will not rouse the God
To clatter heaven with his crackling bolt.
But do not stir the lilies. Feel the ground.
How cool and dark the ground is under us!

SEEPAGE ON A JANUARY NIGHT
for Jean Colleran

I

I feel the waters everywhere seeping into my country
At midnight after the thousand stale blue rooms are finished
And the highway cleared   Only   now and then a truck
Storms by   It is violently gone. The sound of marsh-rushes again.
The meanings everywhere of the waters of the three-days-rain,
   returning.

While I wait for the bus back to New York while I stand under
   a lowrunning sky,
Lit up from below like smoke by the cold wattage of the city
Twenty miles across the bay, the swampgrass along the highway
   is being pushed
Down by the shoving gusts—the cattails, the winter trancing reeds—
And now with the wind stopped they heave back and have become
   intensely motionless

II

I know this land, these eighty or so square yards of asphalt,
This depot (deserted now, with twenty buses, back
   from the commuter runs,
Stabled in hunched sleep back against the big willows).
I know this land: it was a pond and the rain that fell
In the hills to the south—Chapel Hill, Beacon Hill, Red Oaks—

Seeped down through the loam and the pebbly subsoil, down
To the small rushing dark streams that, though sunless, give
   life to the world,
And some of them used to sluice into a marsh pond where
   sumacs and willows
Sucked the wet. And frogs lived there spring and summer
   and in the winter
It was all iced over and once a twelve-year-old boy drowned in it.

III

I feel the waters everywhere seeping through my life
Into the land no longer mine, into the years encased beneath my feet,

Under this asphalt, under this foot of gravel, these several yards
   of fill,
Rock, concrete, incinerated garbage, bulldozed fields
And the trenched faces, that need to be forgotten, of children
   and animals.

Under all this the dark streams seek their deep joining.
I can feel them everywhere in the night. They are unlamenting.
   They are unromantic. They are mud.
They wait for the roothairs of the marsh grass, the frogs' sloughed ova
And, finding nothing, continue strong and ultimate,
To subvert in continuous victory these deathly pavements.

IV

Tonight I understand. Beneath a country frozen for war,
Beneath the frozen daily ritual of the defeat of people
Upon chrome-crustacean plains of days of chambered saharas,
Another freedom works. It was always there. The only final defeat
Is to stand in the depot night of America and not to hear it,

Not to feel through our lives the waters seeping below
   the frost line,
Crumbling the guarded surfaces   breaking out.
Guerrilleros hardly to be dreaded, hardly to be cheered, they are
   now and always
Loosing the jammed strata into dateless insurrection,
The budburst, the chalice of chaos forever hoisted to the sun.

APPARITION

Son regard est pareil au regard des statues,
Et, pour sa voix, lointaine, et calme, et grave, elle a
L'inflexion des voix chères qui se sont tues.

Verlaine, Mon Réve familier

She has come back and I am here again
to be with her in a moment that returns forever.
Alive in heat against a painted sky,
her hair wet out of the sullen bay.

Moving toward me.   her lips unspeaking.
through the packed shimmer of an August day.
and my hands reach and my mouth opens
to make her know me before the end.

While over the masts and the little blue boats
a darkness arches.   A sudden chill and
the sun is a plaque of gold loneliness
on the blackness where the sky caved in.

The shadows in league at the rim of the beach
mount in multiple fold on fold.
Huddled stiffly, they wait for the tide
and for the moment that returns forever.

And even now she is turning, lured
into the doom of my monstrous night.
She walks on the loose sand where the surf
lips her ankles in soft loops. . . . .

and then I must witness again the moment
of the final sea   far out   heaving high
with all the broken loves   the broken loves
upraised on its plunging back

CLARK   Clark Coolidge, born in 1939, lives in Providence, Rhode
COOLIDGE   Island, at the present time. He has worked as a
drummer, a disk jockey, and an editor. His poetry has appeared in An
Anthology of New York Poets, published by Harper & Row. His most
recent book is Space, also Harper & Row.

AMMONIA

garb plant else pack rhythm
sinkers roll organum grape hell
notchers, halvers, REM-hiss, new-add
cork him elm dram obese caustic
sand latch toiler flags
twin dwindle, fels, odds, tool ridge
knaves
   oink squares hatch

while aimer
     dew pod, ash, pawn, likes, preen

gala hack
   snow rain

RODE DINE

scad fury, niner, block
reads in sift banes, psych
sigma add habit, red stairs

 reds

                while

chemo-beamer, coke-gnarl pet grain
dice pine

              sip hush clacker

 pen Sutro histoplasm
                      plan plain

      un peek dump

HOOVER MOOVER

belt putt toe off dead hoove god long dangers shell pot it lids
  knot sticks
a the brick ask is Egypt
                             who some one round whom
      quiet briar dye it giggle
                 ladybird ladder truckloads flower
      the   i
dark 18
            down gold can jello flute sticks shell world
  marge dream
      legs quivers hoof kites
                            flag swell rest
                                signature bounds
the smash THE
          bell put smoke thresh toe
             a first the lab
                        crust sybilant my
lag gyps
        smite tag limey   core the wap
          box bell lubbock mask
      marsh   marsh
   libido onion green bath
                   of watch
      regular signature hates at
            blank oregano stout
                           pure
climb jeep hide bunkom wrap at
             smiler olive stone balloon

squat one draws strung opal flank space dye rout turns bullet
  anger stopper
in crust clips
short there

ALL TALK

in many buildings of them five rows
pure to the those those move
the each course
         and the wait catch
         one dont passes
         to spot pool

one in past print the old other shells
is but over middle of the off appears
      like to do is sit
since ago to even years

on to them to it at all
and when the skim so much as anything
must soon in the widen fast while
notion
        it in an
              all well light
    than true
        some tall

OVER COUNTRY

bright lays lobs spinning house life balloon
coughs
   been spine can humming lieu
sprite bark back node tarot separators
mile cone din onions   horn needles
on victory visitor
to octopi lever flies

scads at mates lard & delves
tang riot owning slim ewes
         coaling
smith to repeat pert to add slat
coiled rip noble & lip rustling
never stone
lank & bent sewn pan lean hairs

BARBARA
DAVIS   Barbara Davis, who was born in 1948, lives in San
Francisco. She is a graduate of Barnard College. Her work
has been published in various literary magazines.

ELEVATORS

elevators
make me
extremely
racist.
i hate
in elevators.
gray old lady
old gray lady
askin me
to hold it
parkinson's disease
takes a halfhour to the door
and then
she wanna
talk
about it.
buddha-heads
callin the place a slum.
the super wants to know
if my man
was invited,
"lots of robberies lately."
goddamnit
I'M
JUST
TRYING
TO
GET
TO
MY
ROOM
white man,
don't ask me
if i'm cold in my short,
short skirt and
try to make me
before the 8th floor
cause i may kill you 'fore the 4th.

SAW OUR PICTURE

saw our picture
on some fine stain glass
no new york dust, just us
pa in his golf hat
& ma in her wig
(weird)
rainin & thundrin
two days straight (no chaser or reefer)
its a big house.
life a double bed with only one body
(satinee) preparee for
thunder, rain on sticky petals/
skin/lavenders greens iris
shiiit!! cracked the sky.
not me, not gonna die
don wanna die, gotta get back to my baby.
the house will breathe when
the rain gives in
i will go
porcelain glaze crackin in the cool
thick sheaths of grey sound-little glaze
crackles
love sweatin wet in no breeze
grey-cracks of thunder getting
1 . . . 2 . . closer to YOU . . . 3.

BLACK GOLD

for Plunky

Black Gold,
we are the richness
we are the balance
of the earth.   the other side of the night
closed petal, shying
dewy til sun opens us
for eyes slipping home.
gold heat of our skin
turned lazing from the brass
and wires
convulsions of machines
staring mirrored into their programming.
no image, digit holes snowing
on parades
chocolated laxative of cities skies.
Black Gold, come hold the warmness of us
heat closeness of our skin
close away from hollow
stairways grey steps clapping
metal down behind coming
up coming up running
down shafts to crowds.
concrete walls tall to fade
into bluegreybrown sky denying
living running down bullets
running bebop
blood throb
shhhhhh pop. shhhhhh pop.
slidin into a crib of cold
shudders and laughs layin
out til the next sweat
Black Gold,
wood cut young to the
flute's desires,   the engravings
are your marks of chiefdom, grave lines
worked in patterns of gods
earth signs
your name Black Gold
your land, the color, your air,
the hum of eyes, hair, touch

Black Gold knowing only the
strangeness of this land of
crushing tunnels, only
passing through Black Gold,
traveling through to
yielding soils, just rained.

S'A BROWN MAN SINGING DOWN

s'a brown man singing down
   the shaft away
a sweet daddy singing his woman maybe
s'a deep voice and I'm alone up
 here peering down windows to
 find a sound i once knew
s'a brown voice down there, full,
   reaching the wholesong coming
   clear where i could run down
   and say man you got some love
   in your voice
cause it's an empty house
   an empty each time is always
and echoes are sold where they've
    been before you
  old rattles playing tricks on new game
    and a man is gone
 old lies and tales clumped dust
 unswept crowding a cold bed
   sunlight on bareness, offwhiteness
the shaft up through
  the empty house
shatters the walls with bangings
 of doings
and glimpses on faces
   and gnarled headed children
and lover brown voices caressing
 unknown empty women.

MY MEMORY IS LONG

my memory is long
my present fulla shit
can ya hold me just a little
   til things get right?
i'm so many things
that don't be in words
the now is too tight
for gittin into it
except you could, well,
the stolen eye is down a tunnel
with itself, time is
always this one
where's the void but what's inside
hold me just a little
   and treat me light.

NINE TIMES SUICIDE EYES

nine times suicide eyes
tryin to draw a shadow while
it moves
violence is forced upon my lines
and i forget
old sunset
weather beaten skies
desert flies
old ivory whatevers
gettin moss every same twenty years
are we all/have we/do any others/
is anybody else tired of bein trite.

GENE   *Gene Fowler, who was born in California in 1931, has had*
FOWLER   *experience as a night-club comic in his native state. At*
present he is a poet in residence at the University of
Wisconsin. Among his collections are Shaman Songs, *published*
by Dustbooks, and Her Majesty's Ship, *published by Grande*
Ronde Press.

VENUS' RETURN TO THE SEA

you go away
turning of necessity
away
turning to the sea

not as rumored
descending
into jade waters
not with shadows
lapping at your eyes
but rising

among harvest waters
on tiptoe
joyously

waters breaking
folding in on the air
you will breathe

your hands
owning responding waters
caressing their lines
into you

these waters are flesh
and now joined

to your flesh

MORNING SONG

folding up my legs
bringing everything closer
to the surface
getting ready to dump
my mind into the lake
prophets are chemists
all the solids must go
into suspension
invite rearrangement
this dance sitting still
the mystic's wonder
seems inhuman
fire-man squatted down
on nickle steel asteroid
dreaming tiny galaxies
this account
a cold white light
flesh to be added
the bone and meat
waiting
knees rubbed sore
and cold
pressed into dew wet
grass
hands blue white
in a cold morning lake
reaching slow motion
for a fish
teeth chattering
early wind running sparks
across my skin
highland lake cut clean
as blue emeralds
raw green sea piling up
white capped rust rivers
of nitric acid on Mars
always the same
mirror
the dance
tears returning

placental fluids
the universal solvent
high plateau sun
tearing apart the atmosphere

from IN THE GARDEN OF MY LADY

III THE DISCOVERY OF A WOMAN

for Jacquie

redwood kings
pine queens, herding smaller breeds
and saplings in a wind stroked orgy
of westward travel over the vulval lips of our coastlands

      it's all a birthing and the torrential nights
        when speech left and spitting singing breakers
          ran over the land

      coastlines forgotten in merging seas
      and a preparation was undertaken
        for these dancing trees
      and their dances

quiet people sitting in a room quietly
fire warmth and visiting
light

these several people
eyes and lower lids in shadow
devil smiles tossed in
to those eyes by old logs that cackle
and snort at these oft tossed
smiles the smilers never see
and the pretty copper haired girl
on the floor by the fire
listens

dark brows entwined and tense over
green eyes flamed
as opals in a temple
poets reading

from burnt umber parchments, scraping
dust away from words poorly remembered
and ancient
cracked shadows hover about the fire

as their tales are retold or mistold
ghost image throats bent and swollen
the heat
of wanting to talk
green
eyes flame with sparks of blue, yellow
molecules
in a young, pulsing brain move
over
gentle flesh is changed
under thin, hiding cloth

among the trees a house
imago mundi
    a singular place of ritual where the initiates
go, most to fail
go   sit   wait
leave wondering at the rustling leaves
in their bellies
when the fall night of the ghosts is done
the night when failed initiates broke vigil
              fell asleep in the house, not knowing
it was a ceremonial house
and ghosts returned to the fire, dying in its embers
with whistled moans and explosive tubercular coughs

i'm going to get a nap
downstairs
and when it's time to go to the city
come wake me
i'll drive everybody to the city

in the room's center
    (ignorant of the girl's departure)
emptied red mountain wine bottles wedged together
a center post
rising to the ceiling, beyond
the ceiling the sky of which the poems spoke
dark with a silver ball of light
rolling its arc

the tales continue, the tellers
yawning, rolling
into blankets, deciding to stay

the city to wait
soon enough the city next afternoon
fire drawing in
a tiny red cluster

        i'll tell jacquie to go to sleep
        we don't need
        a ride to the city

the floors, separate houses
and the outside dark, descending
overgrown hillsides

the girl asleep
her whole body darkened in black clothes
slacks and sweater
a dark corner of the night wrapped around
her
the fire of her hair
gone dark
the vigil above broken
sleep
the wrapping night to be torn away

the touched shoulder turns
brown eyes
are thickets, a dark woods where death
is undiscovered
and gentle furred things run safely
without eyes

       you came, she said later, and that
    she had known me for a very long time, and had waited
      for the time when i would know her

   in a ceremonial house
    ˙ not break the vigil or forget the rituals
       not climb the center post for the easy sky
   but come into the beginning

   pull the real sky
   from where it is coiled in azure strands of lacy
      delicacy
   in the violet embers of her center

when we rose
she had told me the mysteries
promised
                    i am strong   and not greedy

the sun
drew greens from the window framed trees

a magician
discovering similar but unique
rabbits

from HER MAJESTY'S SHIP

XII

'Daphne with her thighs in bark
Stretches toward me her leafy hands'—
Flower child or Moon Goddess, the age
Doesn't matter if young flesh commands,

But darkened eyes spark and reflect,
Go cool and close,
My flesh is old
To her who chose;

Leaves and bark and blossoms
Naturally grow from her,
She wills them not, wills nothing.
Hers is an easy purr:

She sees herself a queen,
Made of dreams, never to die,
And needs Carnival,
Electric heart beat, a dulling lie.

Rock in tiny hand, to throw against
Time, the rock she hears—
Rock and light show trip, break
Time, the rocking years—

There is a terrible oldness in the poet.
Reaching to touch her blossoms,
He draws her eye to death in delicate edges,
Her breasts fill with milk, and dry,
Oldness is contagious.

   .   .   .   .

But darkened eyes spark and reflect,
Go cool and close,
My flesh is old
To her who chose.

DAVID *David Galler, born in 1929, is a widely published poet who*
GALLER *lives, works, and writes in New York City. He has two*
poetry books in print: Walls and Distances *and* Leopards in the Temple,
both published by Macmillan.

THE STONECUTTER'S RESIGNATION

. . . if you will make a man of the working creature, you cannot make
a tool. Let him but begin to imagine, to think, to try to do anything
worth doing; and the engine-turned precision is lost at once. Out come
all his roughness, all his dulness, all his incapability; shame upon shame,
failure upon failure, pause after pause: but out comes the whole
majesty of him also; and we know the height of it only when we see the
clouds settling upon him. And, whether the clouds be bright or dark,
there will be transfiguration behind and within them.

Ruskin, Stones of Venice, Vol. II, Ch. 6.

Though neither of us may understand
My action, sire, I think to leave
These words, which, though they prove no more
Than a strange corner of your uprising
Monument, where lately I thrived
And suffered, are no less. It was
The kind of thing you sought, and even,
If I may say, your manner of treating
All of us who toiled that made
The enterprise, for me at least,
Come down to this.
               I had been used
For years to merely cutting stone
For this or that, given directives
By this land's great masons: I
Was involved with churches, fortresses
And tombs.
          Sire, what could have been
Inside your mind the day you gathered
Cutters and architects together,
The least and best, and said you wished
"A monument." And that was all
You said.
  A monument to what?
To whom? What size? What form? What style?
What kind of stone? And some, the learnèd,
May have considered then (who voiced it
Later): "How long should this thing take?
Establishing *that*, we might attempt
A guess at what we ought to make."
Sire, you had been kind before
That day, and have been ever since,

But walked away.
                    And now to see
Your great builders argue themselves
Weary, who had not had to work
Together before, your humblest cutters
Stare, not having been left before
To their own resources. And then, none spoke—
Just as you left no words beyond
"A monument." As we stood, silent,
It was as though confusion and
Alarming vows had carved of air
Some monument. . .
                    The site was simple.
That is to say, we all managed
To find our ways to a place neither
Too near nor yet too far from where
You'd gathered us. I think some noticed,
Later, it was a place of stone—
Some vast, forgotten temple, an ancient
Shelter, or rubble strangely stacked—
But none so much as had to concern
Himself with transportation save
That of his mind toward doing what
He must, though some, sire, passingly may
Have wondered to what extent our land
Was strewn with stone.
                    That's not for me
To guess, nor you, if I may say,
Considering what has been built and is
Continued. How many hacked their best,
How many knew or thought they knew
What they were doing, is not for me
To say. You passed each day with cool
Encouragement some must have had
The sense to take as kindness; then,
Less frequently. Imperceptibly
Work had quickened (and who will say
Not because of proficiency?):
Most had forgot their homes; few wandered
Except to eat, or rest on nearby
Heaps, or return the stare of whoever
Happened to stare.
                    Sire, I observed
Your master builders build and not

Know when to cease; your cutters carve
(run out of rugged stone) into
What seemed completed. I would not guess
What was complete: the number of minds
And hands, too great; facades and supporting
Structures, one supposed, lay mingled
With fallen fragments—chiseled excess
Or artistry over-reached?—till each
Worked at whatever he could find.
Your stones withstood all work, it seemed,
Though masters came to concentrate
On simplest hewing techniques, and humble
Cutters began to etch such in-
tricacies as may amaze you yet.

As for myself, I would forget.
I would forget the simple shaft
I perfected, all meanings it might be said
To have held; caryatid I carved
Therefrom with little skill; two hand-
locked laid-out lovers hacked from that;
And the great moon-struck splinters watched
All night the night my courage, if courage
It was, fell.
        Sire, you will never know
My name. If some remaining seek
To bear those splinters into your presence;
If any among you choose to call them
A monument, why, you are welcome.

For this is what has come of my hand,
Who had begun to understand.

THE MOUNTAINEERS

for Tony and Rhona in England

In warm weather, they can be seen
descending with makeshift carts
to sell the valley people stone
to repair their houses,
pave streets,
or erect dividing walls
in delicate, good taste;
wood for the coming winter's fires;
homely fruits,
which in their preserved state
are held as luxuries.
Now, what the valley dwellers see
is that these men are coarse:
many the maiden aunt,
who in her youth
was rumored to have paled,
panels her lintel
with wood from the timber line;
many the mountaineer,
who having sold his goods,
gruffly accepted from his host a drink,
got drunk and stayed,
and, toasts later, announced
his wish to buy in town,
but, mortgage signed,
vanished, never to pay.
And, to the valley dwellers' dismay,
their own sons
have traditionally been prone
to rise of a summer's night,
secretly part the grain,
fare up the rocky slopes.
In dead of winter,
laid by a mountain arm
before their fathers' fires,
hearing a sermon
on how valleys extend beyond each peak,
these sons have revived
between faintings to groan:
The heights, the heights!

Many a time,
a man has stood alone
with his son's rescuer
to see him shrug.
Well may he frown:
year after year,
in wizened age
a mountaineer may die;
the valley people
will bear his body to rest
near those of their own,
outside the town,
burial past what he could pay;
and, of his kin,
never has one been known
to object
in any way.

HOPE

Homage and Adieu to Armando Socarras Ramírez

> *Cuban hidden in landing gear survives*
> *flight to Spain at −40 degrees.*
>   —The New York Times, June 5, 1969

According to the American press, the flight
From Havana to Madrid in the unheated,
Unpressurized wheel pod of a jet airliner
Takes nine hours at 29,000 feet.

In three minutes, the doctors say, one loses
Consciousness from lack of oxygen,
And dies soon after; though, if one survive,
It is 40 degrees below zero outside—

With lids clenched, in the wheel pod where you clung
In only a thin shirt, pants, and one shoe,
The American makers of that DC-8
Said one chance in a million existed

That you remain uncrushed when the wheels retracted:
A contortionist might fit himself around
The double gear, hydraulic pipes, and brackets.
The paper noted you were a welder, though—

Who shared your space with a friend, whose body blew
Away in the airstream when the gear was tested.
The paper said you opposed the Communist system.
You spoke fluently from your hospital bed,

But lacked complete coherence as you begged
Not to be sent back. Doctors sighed that construction
Of the pod may well have saved your life.
The pilot's gentle landing at last was credited.

Still, after many days in that sanctuary—
Exposing while it protected—and their insistence,
Dead-pan you told the poised policemen all
The reasons for your flight . . . as wit proposed them.

DICK   *Dick Gallup was born in 1941 in Massachusetts and raised in*
GALLUP   *Tulsa, Oklahoma. At the present time he teaches at the*
St. Marks Workshop on St. Marks Place in New York City. His
collection Where I Hang My Hat *has been published by Harper & Row.*

BIRD LIFE

Birds attack the earth with song
Beady eyes fixed upon a wall
You cannot see

> Each note contributes
> Its iota of energy

The bird within begins the song
Piping it into the air
Surrounding the visual birdie
But it is continuation which reveals beauty
Accent which controls the spark

> Mists desolve about the lamps
> All of an even tenor leading irremissibly
> To human sloth
> The eyes roll from place to place
> Up and down the towers of cloud
> Which haunt the water's edge

> Perhaps we are at sea
> The notes we hear
> Are the first hint of landfall
> And a glass of tea
> The color of dull amber
> On the harbor's brim

And now my sleepy eyes
Rest upon the green
The 43 paces between rough boxes
Guarding the harbor's mouth
Themselves as numb and grey
As the autumnal sea beyond

> Organists of nature blow
> The articulate speech of unknit pipes
> About my ears
> And an absolute unity is assured
> In the broad mantle of the earth's reverberations

CALL IT EGYPT

This is the city of New York
October day chilly wind thin pants
And there are thousands on a bus
Who have been betrayed in the last two hours
Hundreds are taking taxi cabs
Their wives betraying them
Their children disgracing them
Many thousands in the subways
While at home vast orgies unravel
On the waters of the bay
There is a Captain at the wheel
Betrayed ten times monthly
Police cars glide down the streets of Chelsea
Sweet police wives at home in ecstasy
Firemen put out the fire at 413 E. Fifth Street
But their wives are lighting them in Queens
Other women cheat only above the Thirtieth floor

The bookseller married to a City Marshal
Alone has no worries
She's too ugly and has a baby on her knee
She defends American justice
But why not call it Egypt?

WHERE I HANG MY HAT

for Alex Katz

It's like in the art galleries
Where I can see the real thing
Occasionally
                    a classless integrity
Of being
              Huh?
        At last the studio
Lots of toads
                    a birthright
It is a good wrist
        Something to eat
                    a people canvas
I mean paint
              Sunlight
                    a blowtorch
A pleasant and other reckoning with things
Second Avenue or any other
                    blueprint of the future

LIKE THE STARS

Like the stars
I've been wandering a lot

    A paper chair

    The juice begins at home
    And runs uphill toward you
    Clanking away into the mill
    Carrying a clump of broccoli
    My favorite vegetable

    Looking at the ripples on the backs of folks
    Huddled around their mobile homes
    I expect life to be like music

I am bone dry   Sometimes I think you
Bone dry   Are my favorite vegetable

    From the edge of the galaxy
    I puke on the tiny classical heart
    Of Mozart

Little man   Excuse me Mr. Mozart
On the sidewalk   I was aiming for the Crab Nebula

With an Au Pair girl on your arm
A little garden in your ear

        We have good heads you and I
        Though dark rivulets of despair
        Crinkle the grey matter
        And you are not Mozart

The mini-lamp swings through the Earth's core
A twisted
   bent   personality run by an insane conscience
     Balloon night
Underneath a dark cloud of balloons

RELAXATION

So gay on your lovely head
The hat cradles the specialty
Of the house brand new
And hedged with the flowers
Of the past we have somehow
Got through. If night
Should fold in on us
Here in the day dripping
Down the fire-escapes toward
The ground like poetry
In search of the common man
In all things, smokey and
Vapid insight coming near
To what I can't keep my eyes
Off, the fragile jaws
Of antique life, a fretful
Crowd of messages delivered
Long ago in the pouring rain

Then night would find us
As we are, bright lives
Dancing in the somber light
Of history, shiny pencils
At the edge of things.

LIVING TOGETHER

Call up time it's 4:11 AM
Take a chest X-Ray
Spill a glass of H_2O
In honor of the dead

Orange cars
Maroon store-fronts
Blue mail
Red box

The rake is vintage oak
Leaving the garage
Red sun over sodden meadows
Slippery rain washed streets
Shuffling through the Autumn

Seasons are apt
They learn quickly
And pass on
To a higher level

Call up time it's 1970 AD
Kill the children
Put them to bed

YET STILL

Yet still the strange and clotted sea
Runs beneath the morning sun
And leaves us beyond all thought

                              When all the boats are launched
                              And the ship is sinking
                              Then is the time to sing

But the player merely telegraphs his intention
To the interior of the machine
And hence we lack a sense of control
And lose the consonant
Before the breath of music

REALLY MY HEART

Really my heart is a sponge
Aching for the sea (burp) water
To fill it up with Premium
Girls who all have a flooding problem

Terror, death, murder, illness, poverty and rain
Are what bothers me when I have the time
Beans for tonight peas for tomorrow

MARY Mary Gordon, who was born in 1949, lives at Syracuse
GORDON University, where she is working toward her master's
degree and studying with W. D. Snodgrass. She attended Barnard
College.

ON TRYING TO TELEPHONE CALIFORNIA
AT THE BEGINNING OF WINTER

Dearest, around us different weathers flower.
The same sky unbends, but it is not the same.
And when I sleep you stumble from
The restaurant. And when I pull
On morning, you are nodding,
Sliding into some dream town.

Has it to do with money
The beep-beep of you and me
Across the continent?
For love I could not write
An honest word.
Communication is a luxury of impulses
Or dollars I don't have.

Winter sets in its impress day by day.
Cold is a death I thought I could keep off.
I think of how I long for you in cold
And of the times you held my face
In your bare hands, on Broadway, in the zero air.

You say there's no one out there
You can talk to.
                    Speak
To me, my love,
My own, my spotted sun,
Lightest of lights I cannot hide
Or hold, or live by.

TO A DOCTOR

*"Henceforth you shall be fishers
of men"*

They come awash with lore
Of love from its fishbed rising
Sick with longing to be Jonah
Setting up house in some
Warm mammal's mouth.

Poor fish, shimmering sick
With eyes that loom all night. Open.
They bloat to your net.
What is your pull to
Moon, sea,
Gravity, the low, dark kingdoms?

You steer through fog
Lurk in the eel-grass shadows
Lips to the shore, its lap
You whisper under water
Wanting, somehow,
To be friend and fisher
You go calling
Trawling them back
To air, the human element.

NANCY CREIGHTON (1814–59)

It is good work to be the keeper of a grave.
Each new day pulls its load.
The black weeds teethe on earth.
Small branches with the stealth
Of Satan find their way.
What feet have got these
Edgy things in tow?
Each night I leave it clean
Sweet as a child.
But while I sleep
Bad morning lets them by.

John Thomas, my first born.
So long I lay in wait
To see the face that I,
A thrifty sleeve, contained.
I bit my wrist, the sheet
The bedpost.
I did not cry out.
I lay back flat and slack.
Sick of the death
I did not know I bore.

Then Abigail, my girl.
Born in July, her damp hair
Light as flax, clung
Moony to her baby skull.
I watched her life leak out.
I saw it seep.
Half spent by January.
By September, gone.

Joseph, my husband
Stooped now,
Given much to brooding.

I am a small tight bud
That closes on itself.

It is good work to be
The keeper of a grave.

THE DEAD LADIES

for Maureen Sugden

> *"We can sit down and weep;*
> *we can go shopping"*
>   —*Elizabeth Bishop*

What's to be done with death,
My friend?
                We sit
Cross legged, hating men.

Virginia filled her English skirt
With stones.
Always well bred she left behind
Her sensible shoes, her stick
Her hat, her last note
(An apology)
And walked in water
'Til it didn't matter.

We speak of Sylvia
Who could not live
For babies or for poetry.

You switch on Joplin's blues
The room looms black
With what we know
But are afraid to think.

Too scared to say: "and us?"
We leave for work.
Hearts in our mouths.
In love with the wrong men.

QUITE A COMEDOWN

Sodden with sleep
Behind the heavy work
Of love
Release now
Rest, good arm.

Spun out like nylon
Tight blue hearts
Now spill, now spell
What is it
What it is
You mean.

Stripped of all metaphor
Sullen jigging
Still you coat
You swallow up
That itch.

Husked and unlyrical
Sheer, self-centered knot
You do.
You do.

RICHARD   *Richard Hugo, born in Washington state in 1923,*
HUGO   *is an assistant professor at the University of Montana. His*
background includes thirteen years of working for the Boeing Company.
Among his books are A Run of Jacks, *published by University of Minne-*
sota Press; Death of the Kapowsin Tavern, *Harcourt, Brace & World;*
and Good Luck in Cracked Italian, *World Publishing.*

OCEAN ON MONDAY

Here at last is ending
Where gray coordinates with nothing
the horizon wrinkles in the wind.

These will end: shrimp a mile
below, blue shark, sole
rocks alive as crabs in shifting green.

patent bathers, barnacles, kelp that lies
in wilting whips, jelly-
fish that open lonely as a hand,

space that drives into expanse
boredom banging in your face
the horizon stiff with strain.

BLONDE ROAD

This road dips and climbs but never bends.
The line it finally is, strings far beyond
My sight, still the color of useless dirt.
Trees are a hundred greens in varying light
As sky breaks black on silver over and in
The sea. Not one home or car. No shacks
Abandoned to the storms. On one side,
Miles of high grass; on the other, weather
And the sea reflecting tons of a wild day.

The wind is from Malay. Tigers in the wind
Make lovers claw each other orange. Blonde
Dirt rises to recite the lies of summer
Before the wind goes north and cats rip
White holes in the sky. Fields are grim
And the birds along this road are always stone.

I planned to cheat the road with laughter.
Build a home no storm could crack
And sing my Fridays over centuries of water—
Once more, have me back, my awkward weather—
But the land is not for sale. Centuries
Are strung; a blonde road north and south
And no one will improve it with macadam.

The road is greased by wind. Sun has turned
The blonde dirt brown, the brown grass
Black and dark ideas of the ocean
Silver. Each month rolls along the road
With an hour's effort. Now the lovers
Can't recall each other or identify
That roar: the northern pain of tigers

I know that just a word I'll never have
Could make the brown road blonde again
And send the stone birds climbing to their names.

IN STAFFORD COUNTRY

No hills. Raw wind unchecked, brings word
Of death from Texas. No shade. Sun bruises
The oats gold. With homes exposed
No wonder people love. Farms absorb
The quiet of the snow, and birds
Are black and nameless miles away.

Without a shield of hills, a barricade
Of elms, one resorts to magic, hiding
The joker well behind the gesturing hand.
Childish wars continue in our minds.
Paint is the gray it was in Carthage.

Where land is flat, words are far apart.
Each word is seen, coming from far off,
A calm storm, almost familiar, across
The plain. The word floats by, alive
Homes are empty and the love goes on
As the odor of grain jumps in the wind.

J. C. *J. C. Jacobs, who was born in 1945, lives in New York City.*
JACOBS *She attended Smith College and is a graduate of the*
School of General Studies at Columbia University.

CONFRONTATION

Human traffic moving frantic today,
halfthought on thought's heel.
A drunk can't burst the corner crowd's balloon;
a redlight checks the taste,
the dregs of their disgust.
Rag with a paperbag mate,
limps two steps, tugs at his pants,
(knows my face or coat), garbles his request
(his breath, the blur of his face and mine).
Red and breathless, I respond.
The gutters whirl in well-oiled patterns;
street noise quiets. A stifled siren
streams through the fire of the day.

TOUCH AND GO

Beach cots dot the furious shore.
Ladies brush the sea with wishes.
Halfpast the hour of strongest sun,
waiting for hunger, overcome
by sea-air, sand, forced awake
they stare. Waiting, watching
suggestive clouds, important moments
winging in each offshore blow,
sifting sandfleas into patterns
mapping backs of knees and thighs.

Ladies dust the furious shore
inscribing visions with fingertips.
On sandbar islands of lowering tide
their human voice outcries the gulls'
vying for ripples of sandspaced air.
The water's rush, expressed in lulls.

ACTIUM, 31 B.C.

The sky flashes dreams;
doves linger or take flight.

Antony: My biographers are fickle
as they said she was.
I, all politician, lover,
am invincibly soldier.
I add no balance to their
accounts. She, no more
Egyptian queen than I,
freedman. More a matter
of the senses. We lived
to decimate, and so forth.

Cleopatra: Dionysius, Isis are to blame.
Caesarion first, diverting
the Nile flow into my heart.
It is said a Ptolemy should distinguish
what is greed from what is heart.

THE RECLUSE

She sits embroidering them,
those spots of mind
where darkness kinks.
Her privacy, a quiet room
to pace in now the going's done.
Sewing empty flowers, their
blooming outlines threaded
shaky as her pulse, she senses
how the outside evening deepens,
when the hour women weep
arrives, departs. She
adjusts her lamp and fixes tea;
she'd eaten early. A warm
sip and she sighs out over silence.
Her eyes lightly close
on wallpaper ovals,
like the hoops of years,
vacant, trimmed with roses.
She circles round the rim of pain,
loops a stitch, mechanical,
and circles round again.

FREE WILL

Stripping a chicken to its bone,
dividing flesh from sentiment.
The ripped skin stretches like a winding sheet.
This flabby time tastes raw, oracular,
as if with twists of cartilage revolve the turns of fate.

A dull streaked blade
jabs, slashes, stabs, retreats.
Its slick tip penetrates
phalangeal strings of reddened meat
hung from a whitened joint.

Cat eyes me hollowly,
her wishes dry my throat.
She cries. I leap.
My insides dart
startled to the bloody heart.
Divined by accident.
She cries. I leap.
I reproach her innocence.

JACOB AND THE ANGEL

It used to be. . .
the last time I came by
this way . . .
(I will not let thee go)
its hot head lay
invisible
beside this sinew
of a vein
(except thou bless me),
breath, a stinging covenant.

Abyss of angel wrestles
time men synchronize
a watch by
(I will not let thee go),
gropes to see
the living skull
laid there
(except thou bless me)
beside that very vein.

RICHARD *Richard Kostelanetz, born in 1940, attended Brown*
KOSTELANETZ *and Columbia universities and now lives*
and works in New York City. He is best known for his extensive critical
writings and anthologizings.

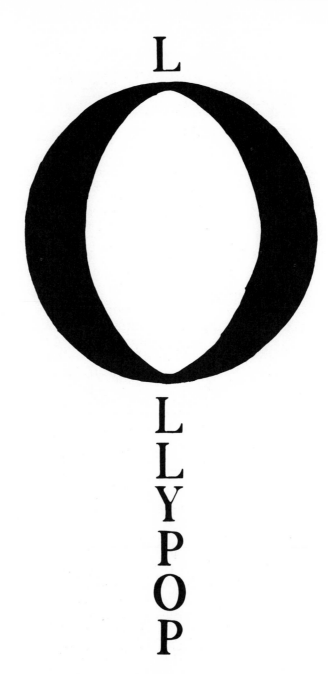

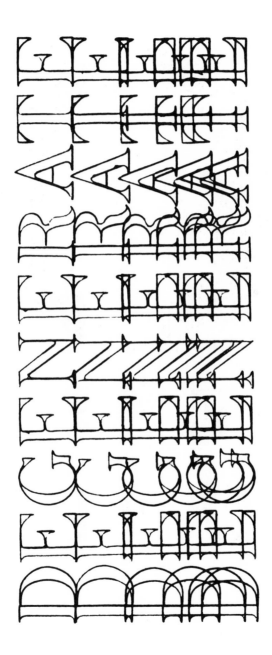

INTEGRATION

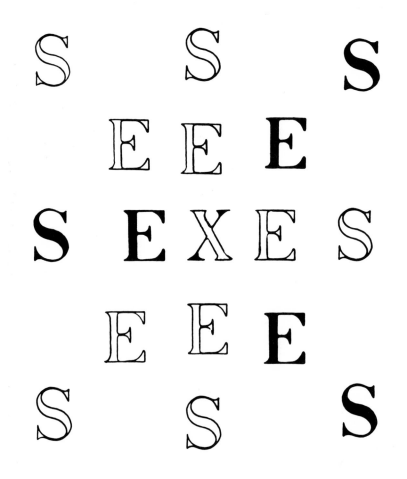

SERIAL POEM--TWELVE-TONE ROW

For Milton and Sylvia Babbitt

white	ivory	beige	ochre	brown	khaki	olive	hazel	green	azure	mauve	black
IVORY	BEIGE	GREEN	OLIVE	HAZEL	KHAKI	BLACK	AZURE	MAUVE	WHITE	OCHRE	BROWN
WHITE	IVORY	HAZEL	KHAKI	OLIVE	BROWN	MAUVE	AZURE	GREEN	BEIGE	BLACK	OCHRE
OLIVE	HAZEL	BLACK	OCHRE	GREEN	IVORY	BEIGE	BROWN	KHAKI	MAUVE	WHITE	AZURE
GREEN	AZURE	OCHRE	BEIGE	IVORY	WHITE	BROWN	OLIVE	HAZEL	KHAKI	MAUVE	BLACK
HAZEL	GREEN	WHITE	IVORY	BLACK	OLIVE	KHAKI	OCHRE	BEIGE	BROWN	AZURE	MAUVE
AZURE	MAUVE	BROWN	BLACK	GREEN	KHAKI	IVORY	OCHRE	OLIVE	HAZEL	BEIGE	WHITE
OCHRE	BROWN	MAUVE	IVORY	BEIGE	BLACK	GREEN	KHAKI	WHITE	HAZEL	AZURE	OLIVE
KHAKI	OLIVE	IVORY	MAUVE	WHITE	AZURE	OCHRE	BEIGE	BROWN	BLACK	HAZEL	GREEN
BROWN	KHAKI	OLIVE	MAUVE	OCHRE	WHITE	BLACK	GREEN	AZURE	IVORY	BEIGE	HAZEL
BEIGE	OCHRE	AZURE	GREEN	MAUVE	IVORY	WHITE	BLACK	BROWN	OLIVE	HAZEL	KHAKI
BLACK	WHITE	OLIVE	BROWN	KHAKI	HAZEL	GREEN	MAUVE	IVORY	OCHRE	AZURE	BEIGE
MAUVE	BLACK	KHAKI	OCHRE	BROWN	GREEN	HAZEL	OLIVE	WHITE	AZURE	BEIGE	IVORY

J. L. *J. L. Ledbetter, who was born in Illinois in 1934, now lives*
LEDBETTER *in California, where he is an assistant professor*
of English at California Lutheran College. He has several chapbooks in
print and has been published in literary journals around the nation.

SOME SIGN OR DREAM

They gathered on a Tuesday to read the sign
telling them to get off their land:

>500 Mi. S.E. Govt. Land.
>Gd. Housing, Running water,
>Tract 158, See Gus Gerth.

They grunted . . . one laughed
and spat into the black dirt —
    some stayed to read the words again —
    going over and over the letters to suck from them
    some sign or dream. . .

the rest withdrew, formal,
like an odd parade —

>some stood apart
>their thumbs hooked in SEARS jeans
>trying to follow the winding blue water
>in the tall grass
>as the prairie rolled away to the Southeast.

THE HOME

The hot morning sun
sucked the shadow
off the wide-board porch where the old
woman   rocked;
the bustle in the house
was noisier than necessary
but she rocked the same for all of the talk
that hung heavy on the August air.

From her porch she could see the ladies
gather across the graveled street, their heads
bonneted and bent in the trellis shade.

    Her long bony hands tightened
    on the smooth brown rocker arm;
    she shuffled her feet on the porch
    and lifted a yellowed handkerchief
    to her throat, then let it drop
    in her lap.

The sun spun in a mazy light
white motions in the beams that struck
    the hot roof of the pickup that
bumped the ditch and rolled to a stop
at the porch. . .
    the driver smiled a wide
    clean smile and said
        "Mam"
    as he leaped the steps and banged
    through the screen door;

the old lady tried to say something . . .
as he jumped the steps, but he moved
too fast in the sun, his face blurred in the
web of years that held her in her chair—

    The ladies in the shade
    looked up as the family
    started out the door, formal,
    like an odd parade;

they marked the ties, the old
blue suit, the fans, the brooch,
and how they passed the chair but
turned in awkward angles to look before
they got in cars.

    The old woman rocked
    and rubbed one hand upon
    the   other;
    and felt she ought
    to tell them of her dresses
    that they folded in the truck —
and the ladies on the swing
cried "hush", and "come out
and see now" to others in the
house across the street —

    the son came up the steps,
    the chair rocked, but slower;
and turning once, she saw the neighbor's
cat lying quiet in the gladiolas watching
the soft brown birds dancing in the
bird bath —
    and she kept looking at the cat
    and the birds as she lifted from
    the chair, her back held firm
    by long strong arms;
    her head against his chest — the world
    moving around her as she
    watched —

    and all the world there was
    sat quiet across the street
as the trellis vine stirred slightly
in the darkness of the porch.

I-80

  runs along the Blue River
and the hot station wagons boil over beneath the
diseased Elms that bear the red X.

    (Next year we're promised Pin Oaks
    croons the elderly lady passing out
    brochures.)

The river is green from the trees—
    green and thick—
    slow moving between the muddy banks.

        The Plaque reads
      Prehistoric Indian Site

"God, all they got in Nebraska is dead Indians?"
(says a man in shorts with black dress shoes
and long black socks)

        "Skeeters!"
  (slap—whack—with the brochure on red necks)
    "hell, let 'em keep the place. . ."
             and off on I-80
    heading East to education
    or West to retirement—
        leaving the Blue sluggish
  in its banks
      and the OTO bones
      quiet beneath the green hillock.

THE WOODS

Those branches, there . . . did they move?
    stand close awhile, soon or late
it might be there again. I'll prove
    to you these woods can hear: shhh, wait!

There. It made the noise: I heard
    it move; some subtle shift of shade
beneath the branch. You say a bird.
    I say something else, some sound nature made

for us, just because she wanted to.
    You needn't look at me;
if you want a name, "bird" will do:
    I know what I saw. And see.

PHILIP   Philip Levine, a resident of Fresno, California, is an
LEVINE   assistant professor of English at Fresno State College.
Among his books are Not This Pig, published by Wesleyan,
and 5 Detroits, published by Unicorn Press.

THISTLES

for George Oppen

A MOUNTAIN THISTLE IN MARCH,

the stem a bitter green,
the blossom faded
like the stained robes
of martyrs.
            Roots
spun through entrails
of the wakened earth
darkening into rocks
and the long nests.

The sun up long
past five, hanging
in a crown of gold.
—Take the mountain thistle—
it said.
           A film of snow
whirling from the thickets,
the new throats
of my fingers
streaked and itching.

IT'S AUGUST.

Dust sifts from the dark wings
of the magpie, the trails
flounder in sand.
A high wind in the tips
of the pines,
            without
a sigh the leaf on
my palm dies
into itself.
Somewhere
           on this mountain
a truck gears down
and the rocks flake
into smaller and smaller lives.

I CLIMBED NINE FENCES THIS MORNING

haven't seen a cow or goat or horse or man. . .

In the center of a long meadow
try to sit still
the patient rocks staring
the sun stopped in
the pines assembled at the far edge
listening

Each time I lean my weight
on the top strand
something in me tears loose

How do I get out?

IF HE RAN

his long hair would fly
in the wind, if he sat still
his mind would run
with the names of rocks and trees
turned against him.

23yr old draft dodger
he tracks the rim
of this sullen mountain lake.
He sent his girl away
he watched his
Whitman, Rilke, Snyder
go up with the boathouse
a bright showering cage
against the night sky.

He feels the corners
of his mouth pull down,
his eyes vague.
Some old poet
would say, Bereft.
He thinks, Up Tight,
Fucked over, trying to walk
inside my life.

IN THE CITY OF MY BIRTH

someone sees my eyes
and turns from the mirror
someone hears my voice
and shouts and shouts
to keep it out

At noon through the vacant squares
the sirens breathe
shuddering in each life
I lost

In the room I forgot
which I said I'd never forget
the mended bathrobe slips
to the floor,
the closet sags
with the sudden weights
of regret

The middle-aged press operator
curls on my bed
in his leather jacket
In the shadows
of the struck elm
the sparrows hush

Above, on the 4th floor
the Appalachian widow
sings into the sink
until her sons come one by one
to take the trees apart.

DOWN THE MOUNTAIN

in Fresno, L.A., Oakland
a man with three names and no features
closes my file.
                    The winds
are weighed, the distance clocked.
Everything is entered in the book.

HANGING ON IN THE MOON SOIL

north of Alicante
where even the rocks
can no longer sleep,
          the cactus
dreams on the promise
of rain.
        Little pagan
villages of green spines
tenements of earthly joy.

And here and here
a thistle
like a fox leaps
toward the burning
filaments of shade.

THEY GO ON HITTING

flies and grounders.
The darkness rises
from the long grass
and pulls them in.

The last raw plume
of day breaks up
and flares out, when I
look back there's no one,
only a dark sea—

Somewhere out there
forests of antennas,
empty houses, trees, posts,
dead cars, all
the closed presences
of this world—

And the voices of kids
floating out and back.

My wife and I
stand wordless

on the chilled lawn
waiting for our sons
to come as they please,
to step suddenly out
of nothing, still warm,
grass smeared, robed
in their own songs.

THE BIG GUY RAN AND HID HIMSELF

in the can, and Mez and I
stayed and fought. Their drunkenness
uglier even than ours, their bodies
marvellous and no imagination to pull
their punches.
            Upright to the hospital,
the shabby dignity of losers
who fought for nothing
and deserved everything we got.

                        7 years
later the big guy, rabbit-eyed
at quiet New York drink party,
shook my hand.
            Friend, I didn't say,
we get our chance, it comes
round and it
comes round. Those twitch-nosed
academic pants-pisser poets
of the 50's will take up
against the State,
and you'll be with us,
Mother.

    RISES IN THE DARK

fixes coffee
hands moving like starlings
above the glowing electric rings

Outside a mockingbird snaps
from the sycamore
the branch sways
and calms

60 year old wanderer
he sits in the dark
in my chair, plotting
the next move, the poem

—Tool & Die past,
L.A. backyard cabinetshop
& no loyalty oath,
8 yrs Mexico woodlathe—

Always a new dark
the cup nests in the stained hands
the mockingbird returns
the tree returns.

THE DAWN FOX

high on the meth of
drugged chickens
attacks dogs, gophers, hoses,
tricycle tires.
                If they knew
he was here they'd hunt
him on horseback among
the abandoned cars
in The Hollywood Hills'
Wilderness, they'd
make a game of it
drinking his death in
Pepsi,
      his death who rode
the shield of Luca up the impossible
Etruscan slopes, who turned
to fight the pig mounted Archers
of the Moon.
             Tearing his
yellowed eyes through the screen door
to get the house cat.

THE THISTLE

torn off and brought down,
admired
and tossed on a shelf

All night the jets hammering
above the house
all night the thistle
opening and opening.

and now the first sun
flooding

everyone breathing
his own life

the house living

the refrigerator's
even pulsing
the water heater
yawning and
popping

the east windows
rubbed
open on the quicksilver
of the eucalyptus

Not snow but
seeds fallen
through the roof
of my life
on the stained table
the glass
the silent phone
the unanswerable letter.

AUTUMN

Out of gas south
of Ecorse. In the dark
I can smell the dogs
circling behind the
wrecked cars.
                    On a sidestreet,
unlighted, we find a
new Chevy. I suck
the tube until
my mouth fills
and cools with new
American wine.

Old man says,
Elephant moves slow, tortoise
don't hardly move at all and they
has no trouble to be
a hundrid.
                    The small
ladders of hair dangle
from his nostrils, hands
peppered like old eggs.

I left you in Washington,
honey, and went to Philly. All the
way beside the tracks, empires
of metal shops, brickflats, storage tanks,
robbing the air.
                    Later, behind
barbed wire, I found small arms
swaddled in cosmoline, tanks, landing
craft, half tracks smiling
through lidded eyes,
grenades blooming in
their beds.
                    April,
1954, we've got each other
in a borrowed room.

Who comes before dawn through
the drifts of dried leaves
to my door? The clawed gopher,

the egret lost on his way, the inland
toad, the great
Pacific tortoise?
                        I rise
from a warm bed and go and
find nothing, not a neighbor
armed and ready, not a cop,
not even my own son
deserting.
                I stand
in a circle of light, my heart
pounding and pounding at the door
of its own wilderness.

Snow steaming on the still
warm body of the jackrabbit
shot and left, snow
on the black streets
melting, snow falling endlessly
on the great runways that
never fill.
                    The twentieth autumn
of our war, the dead heart
and the living clogged
in snow.
                A small clearing
in the pines, the wind
talking through the high trees,
we have water, we
have air, we have bread, we have
a rough shack whitening,
we have snow on your eyelids,
on your hair.

HOW MUCH CAN IT HURT?

The woman at the checkstand
Who wishes you cancer

The fat man who hates his mother
The doctor who forgets

The soup bubbling on the back of the stove
The stone staring into the sun

The girl who kisses her own arms
The girl who fries her hair

The egg turning brown under the spoon
The lemon laughing all night long

My brother in his uniform over Dresden
The single thrill of fire going for the bed

The kindergarten blowing its windows out
Chalk burning the little fingers

The newspaper waiting all weekend
Dozing in rain with the deaths smeared on its lips

The oiling and the loading and the springing
The bullets sucking quietly in their cradles

How much can it hurt in the wood
In the long nerve of lead, in the fattened head

How much can it hurt
In each ration of meat hooked and hanging

In the unfinished letter, the dried opened socket
The veil of skin flapping, the star falling

My face punctured with glass
The teeth eating themselves in dreams

Our blood refusing to breathe, refusing to sleep
Asking the wounded moon

Asking the pillow, asking, asking
How much can it hurt?

ROBERT

October. From Simpson's hill
the great moon of stone
frowns in the rain. In the
fields below dark bruises
of spike stiffen into seed.
The cows are shuffling
behind me, back down
to the long chromium sheds
and the painless taking.

I watch an hour pass.
The darkness rises from
the floor of the valley
thickening the air between
branches, between stone
and tree, between my eyes
and what was here.

Now I'm in the dark.
I remember pages torn
from an automotive catalogue,
an ad once fallen from
heaven and hanging in
the city air—"It's never too late . . ."
If I follow my hands
will I feel the winter shake
the almonds into blossom?

¡HOLA MIGUELIN!

I

The night is rising in the young grass—
before noon and the land wind
sways through the fields. Along the trunk
of each blade, a juice rising
toward the pale crown.

I shut my eyes and imagine
a black dried bough of olive.
I bend it. When it gives
with a dry cough
a fine dust rises into our nostrils.

II

She stumbles into the noon—this morning
she was a shy wife—and the young
coarse wine that numbs
her arms and cools the sweat on
her forehead is summer itself.

If she goes forward she does so
from side to side
on her long delicate legs, bearing
herself between them, a faint
musk, a crown of curls, a gift
for the night that is always rising.

GARY Gary Livingston, who was born in 1943, lives in New York
LIVINGSTON City. He attended the University of Oregon, and
is now a free-lance writer. His work has been seen in many literary
magazines, and he frequently gives public readings.

HOMECOMING

We sat in cantilever forest.
I took gifts of needles and cones.
Lichen rocks I gathered on White
for the struggle home.
"I was up twelve-thousand feet . . ."
and they fell asleep.
They had a heat wave and dead cops
and baseball was out of control.
The subways were hotter than baked sage,
streets split cleaner than frost-wedged stone.
Smog was sand and sky sucked land
and no horizon stayed the hand.
Do you hear? No. Annual reports
flood tides, slumping stocks
strip mountainsides. The rocks
tell my desk, we are older than you,
but here that doesn't matter,
like dying nuns in Grand Central
or the ragpicker passed
or pigeons prying bread
from bone.

PATTERNS

All the mistakes, the restlessness
at remembrance, the formless
nights, no embrace or demarkation,
no sleep or wakefulness, no dreams
to pace regeneration,
all the patterns regrouped,
crystalline, always the same,
each segment the same,
each fate catenulate,
the body bound,
each nexus the next,
sleep's not found under blankets
or breaths, each door unopened
leads to death's,
each plangent fragment frees
the depths, each sleep uncaught,
like love, the last.

LOWER EAST SIDE BLOCK PARTY

I (THE INVITATION)

We all embark on journeys daily,
work, the market, candy stores,
the park, across a splash of streets
where stink completes el barrio;

flora and fauna change with each stride
to mutation of familiarity, the green
we greeted at the door is brown
farther down the block
where manpacks of rats
rummage flesh at night
and shadows cringe
at the bite;

it is afternoon,
I am going home to my soul.
Ninth Street encounters
Tompkin's Square where drum beat
the Virgin Islands, Haiti,
Puerto Rico, palms on the beach,
the fair trades sweet, and hurricanes
in September

I find you curled up,
stoking your coals
on shoals of sidewalk,
across the street from a continent
of drum beat, drugs
and dance,
you walk up sensing my rhythm
and irrationality,
see fire in the water of my face,
reach out,
touch white ectomorph
and elegy of race;

beyond you the buildings line up
in commotion of brick
and you invite me to the dot

I had always seen as illusion
                          of perspective
that is your block.

II (PREPARATIONS)

We find our own ways
through poppycock of days,
with rifle and mortar
or mortar and brick,
with exploit and influence
or confluence of image,
with dance and re-dance
or redoubt of room,
with crepe and cardboard
and catatonia,

here on the Lower East Side,
where a river divides the dialectic
and heaven and hell are concepts
of other neighborhoods,
we prepare what's left of the day
for Ascension,
roll back the stone from poverty's
tomb, rejoice
what we do not have this year,
anoint ourselves
with conga-sweat consecration
of body, bind our blood
on the fingertips of minds;
it is written in the Books
that we shall dwell together
whosoever contribute to brotherhood,
and beer;

the nun
guards our holy checkpoint,
can banish cops with a flash
of cross,
hosts of neighbors, in second front,
seize windows. We wait,
rapacious for Saturday night. Overhead,
the banners of our defiance

flap between landscapes
of fire escapes
like summer birds
caught in a calm
of memory.

III (NO BACCHANALIA)

Dionysus isn't here;
the poetry escapes the godly ear.
The prisoners await their year,
the faithful, shackled, dance
in mimic wine-step.
No one sneaks past judgment
pledging honor to gods
either living or dead;
our theater is precinct sacrosanct,
our poetry policed and bled.

My view is over conga drums
and from within their resonance;
past their hips, my thoughts find form
boom cracka tap out the hole in the end
and into the street where sleek cars
crouch as paupers' props,
souls lost to devils of
dealership,
buildings tilting, sun-crazed
and leading in sullen array
to the modern high-rise
an infinity away.
The street becomes blare of beat
submerging all hunger,
the stoops spill happy rinds of people,
the weekend squeezes a sonorous climax:

muchachas walk by,
breasts dancing, legs in love-stride
that could break a Pope's heart,
lips full like Iphigenia's on the way
to Achilles,
turning to death on this altar

of stench
though their hearts go on beating
boom cracka tap
and the breasts go on dancing
to the postludes of pageants
that never existed.

IV (WAITING FOR VALDEZ)

Valdez, Valdez!
You spoke of mucho corazon
and the brotherhood of flesh and bone,
of your own heart towering
over tenements in a reach
morality envies,
of the battle that befell
the party's knell, and the army
that restored corrupt propriety,
of the secularizing nightstick blows,
of your own bare brother
winning trial by truncheon
in chaos of August evening,
of the space and the cramp
and the pigeons that give you wings . . .

You are more a man
than any seafarer who ever plied
a dream, and drunk, you are stagger
to all successes ever dared,
and gold, more malleable soul
than any currency ever stamped,
and wise, more wine than ever
rested philosopher's mind,
and justice, more fire than all
man's hells conspire,
and love rolled up in black oblique
where one must beat the animal
to discovery,

and on this night-soaked stoop
I await your hour, justice,
rhymes of men, deliverance,

deluge, rivers of blood, descent,
rejoicing, the parting of seas
and their fold,
as the wind searches streets for truth,
and paper is caught up in a burning bush
of swirl.

V (THE LONG WALK HOME: A RECOLLECTION)

It always comes back,
the long walk home,
the hours I cannot recapture
but trust more than those
I approach,
the slums that dissolved
into whitewash far down the block
where some say civilization begins
but doesn't any more than wars
end just because God
is watching,

the buildings that were higher
than the slum-sky ever arched on
                              sparkling days,
and were surpassed by arrogance alone;
the stoops that convened no quorum of revelers,
the trees that were fuller west
of Fourth Avenue, coming to fruit at Fifth
and decaying again farther down
from some lack in the excrement
of slumdogs,

and nobody cares what the trees
are doing, how the leaves turn brown
a little earlier each season,
and soon they will back up clear to spring
and be gone forever.

LOUIS   *Louis Phillips was born in 1942. A graduate of Stetson*
PHILLIPS   *University, he lives, teaches, and writes in New York*
City. He has published two fairy tales: The Man Who Stole the
Atlantic Ocean, *Prentice-Hall; and* The Secret Voyage of Melvin
Moonmist, *Jarrow.*

RUS IN URBE

Rus in urbe,
plants in my apartment die,
brown leaves scattered on the rug,
planters turned upon the sill.
I shall not set foot again
in that mountain city
where my wife was raised,
a country girl with city longings. . . . .

Rus in urbe,
a foreign phrase rolls
in a foreign season
where city climates take their toll.
5 floors up, I sweat out
a small drought, one marriage
gone to pot, one pepper plant
gone to seed, one geranium
trampled underfoot. Water
in the tub is not quite a pond,
bears no resemblance to that gorge
near my wife's city
where pines suspend the afternoon
& boulders tempt the climber
from the fall's edge.
Rus in urbe. 5 flights up,
I sweat out my own uprooting.

A METAPHOR CARRIED ALMOST TO EXCESS

Let grief be as bone
& mend as bone,
Fibers intertwining
As we once intertwined.

What is often broken
Often heals,
& sometimes stronger
At the join & feels

Solid as if it carries
Greater weight,
Growing firm
At the tissues' bite

In the jagged vertebrae's
Links & heals.
Who would know
A sorrow lest he feels

It to the bone,
Stiff grief
& marrow
Of this life

In constant rending.
Let grief be as bone
That we grow strong
In our mending. . . .

SEQUENCE FOR MY LADY

Half this dancing
Is my own;
The floor, well-honed
Gives back my steps,
Much doubling
& redoubling here,
Heel on wood,
Toe on stone,
Half this dancing
Is my own.

Blessed by they
Who play
The beast with two-backs,
Motion back & forth
In circular dilemma;
By moon, by sun,
We die,
That school-boy pun
Most of us have known.
Half this dancing
Is my own.

Who said that we'd be one
Told lies,
Or that my bed would cure
Her faults & mine;
Who ever thought
It heaven
Or that our kisses
Would be even?
But leave her faults alone.
Half this dancing
Is my own.

What face here
Is bared for me to kiss?
Lips that cry,
Eyes that speak
A rhetoric of tears,
Hands that lead

My flesh to come.
My, how I've grown!
Half this dancing
Is my own.

AKKO

"80,000 crusaders died
    taking this city
in a two-year siege."
Either that
or the generals lied

& gave a wrong body count.
Perhaps
it was another city
entirely. I, at least,
admit
that's possible. But, if so,
may all their souls mount

To heaven
for such a valiant siege;
2 years gone
from their ladies' beds,
2 years away
from night-gowns
& perfumes, all the solid comforts
that their Christ ultimately win.

Today, I cannot remember
exactly
what country
Akko's in,
but I am certain
it is a strong city,
that its streets are straight,
that its doors
open to strangers,
that its walls & gate
rest upon firm foundations,
pleasant in summer,
temperate in December.

Far be it from me to speak
of burning oil,
pitch & totter of the ladders,
arrows that wavered,

spears that broke, the smell
of the open privies
where even saints
emptied their bladders
& the spotless took a leak.

Such descriptions are beyond my range.
Instead,
I point to the Akko sun,
white parasols
opened like beaches,
barbaric children
grinning with hunger,
dots on a very human map,
awaiting almost any kind of change,

Any kind of seasonal shift & shake.
"80,000 crusaders died
      taking this city
in a two-year siege."
Either that
or the historical cartographers made
a very common mistake.

LOVE & THE TELEPHONE COMPANY

At first we ran up bills
Dialing long distance,
Until I was down to nickels
& dimes, but ready to pounce

Upon the phone when it rang,
Hoping it might be her,
Thankful for any metallic tongue,
Waiting for a static offer

Of reconciliation. *Sorry*
Your call did not go through.
Often when I dialed in a hurry,
I dialed a *9* instead of zero:

The number you have dialed
Is not a working number,
& many times the dimes failed
To come back & I had no more

Change & yet was whipped up
Into a fury to make my call.
Sorry. If you please hang up.
There were nights I'd walk all

Over Manhattan to find a phone,
One not ripped apart,
An instrument whose line
Had not been cut for sport.

Hoodlums wreck telephone booths
For sport in Manhattan. They
Could care less about a truth
Dying to be spoken—pay

Phones all over Manhattan
With the dials ripped off,
The change box pried open
By some 2-bit punk, a tough

Who doesn't need to call
To see if his wife's all right.
But tonight is a night in April,
& I am at a new phone, a white

One with a long cord, & I tell
The operator my wife's number.
I am calling my wife & the smell
Of another woman is on my fingers. . . .

78 MINERS IN MANNINGTON, WEST VIRGINIA

Thanksgiving. They have
taken a sample
of the air,
have found ample

evidence of Carbon Monoxide.
Somewhere
in that air
there are
78 miners. If they are alive,
it is a miracle,
& no one will save
them now. It is a simple

matter of sealing off the mine
to stop the fires
& the explosions. The wives
knew it all along,
it comes with the territory,
but found it impossible

to admit to themselves.
News comes frequently
from the Mannington, West Va.
mine, but there are no rumors.
Over the clotheslines,
white ropes dividing
the air with parallel lines,
women with stringy hair
refuse each other's mornings.
Their wooden clothespins are
held tight in their lips;
The dungarees shake out
their knees and pivot slightly;
early morning dew
keeps the sheets damp.
But there are no rumors.

Day after Thanksgiving. A new
explosion rocks the mine.

Some say this is not a poem,
but what does that have to do
with the 78 dead miners
of Mannington, West Virginia?

BEGINNING A NEW DECADE AT MY FRIEND'S HOUSE
IN PENNSYLVANIA

Awakened by crystal,
Ice clattered
On my friend's roof,
The afternoon
Broke its heaven
On his walls. As if
Mouse feet

Our temperature squeaked;
A fist of ice
Upon the door
Lulled us from our sleep.
Farther up,
Wild geese croaked,
Brown feathers
In a pale sky.

2.

Every year
It's the same thing,
A satchel of promise,
A packet of resolution,
A setting forth
In a thousand directions
At the same time.
Lights on the horizon,
Fire on the landscape,
A single hearth
To be warmed by.

3.

Today I am deliberate
As ice, as air.
Amid the Pennsylvania farms
I make this prayer:
That I piss warm
& all of us
Be safe from harm.

4.

If his house
Were a castle,
I would say
The blackbird
Walked the tower.

If his house
Were a peasant's hut,
I would say
Deer sniffed at the door.
If I came
Upon his house
In any direction
I would say
Let me in, let me in.

DAVID   *David Posner lives part of the time in California, part of*
POSNER   *the time in England, and part of the time in France. In*
California he has taught at San Fernando Valley State College.
His poems have been widely published.

DIALOGUE WITH THE COUNTESS

Swelling his sacs
Mauriac croaked: Daisy,
a tower with an interior staircase.
We climbed to get nearer the sun.
She rouged her cheeks so quickly
it reddened the tip of her nose;
believed in losers, fell for flattery.

    I faced uphill, the sea at my ears.
    Crickets sang from her forest.
    Thickets were narrow,
    elms to the third bend.
    Her pavilion threw sand in my eyes,
    musk, clay from the eaves.
    Why were the shutters sad?
    A fountain sprayed the bricks.
    I swung a nail-studded door, caught
    Daisy weeping into a mirror.
    She stretched the long-stemmed roses an octave.

"Dear friend, if you're loved,
you win in the end."
"Rococo or not, one learns to make a fuss.
Even the Duchess was victorious
painting her portrait of
Valery among ambassadors."
"Snobs fly from question to question with
a faint suggestion of death, their words
are like a migration of birds."
"I notice order in each flight:
for my trouble pride
is sensible, elaborate."
"A handsome gesture's all I tried
between footfall and snowfall."

    The country around here dedicated
    to bulldozers
    grows villas in the suburbs, *mon rêve, mon repos.*
    Our ghosts haunt city houses
    (the ceilings higher).

Ned, *enfant terrible* at fifty,
   met you at the door, composing like Poulenc.
   "But never failed a hostess, *mea culpa.*"

They sobbed when Kathleen Ferrier sang Orfée
to match Marie Blanche's delicate perfume
on Thursdays after Monteverdi:
complicated lesion of her brain
drifting unconscious six months before she died;
George Ernest played dirty songs
in his only clean suit, thinking
dear God, look, an empty barrel.

   "Landscapes without figures? Even *those*
   suffered the triumph of a few amenities
   (Madame de Stael: the only view of Naples
   from my hotel window). An apple's what
   Matisse paints in this room.
   Nature was a boom invented on the Stock Exchange.
   I arrange with God to breathe."
   "Your friend the Viscountess
   digesting her men inside her evening dress?"
   "A thirsty landscape makes a lot of noise.
   I see peace spread on my grass,
   if I could pay for it."
   "The price defeats your fashion
   like Marie Louise's German boys,
   fruit of her unfelt compassion."
   "The *petitis fours* they serve in hell?
   Ennui is very French. It does as well as
   standing at the foot of the Cross.
   I have such bills to pay!"
   "How much did you give for
   incurable bachelors who gape like open wounds?"
   "One can't escape his war!
   Bebe took a curtain
   and then
   dropped dead."

No hidden glades: no bronze lions but ours,
no dignity except
on hoofs of champion horses from Camargue.

We taught the scene good manners.
The afternoon stiffened to attention, twilight
condescending but not familiar;
evergreens wet in the driest summer,
dry after rain:
an elegant perversity.

>"I wanted my hedges trim, my silver fresh
>though I had to pay the butcher cash,
>give up Jacques Heim for the Bon Marché.
>Always fatter in the evening
>I told myself, Daisy, don't eat
>(Boris throwing his arms around my bottles:
>'Diaghilev, I'll mount a ballet bigger than this house.')"

"Bigger than your taxes?"
"What seasons we played!
I tuned my Limoges:
le Stagione."
"Did liars turn to crystal
because a flute was flawless?"
"In a world of diamonds
every stone reflects the light."

>*Midsummer Night's Dream* inside her woods:
>she threw Shakespeare at the Nazis like a lemon pie,
>plop! in their faces.
>The courage of her lawn became a proverb,
>extravagance keen enough to be Virgilian.
>"Would you enjoy being called (I'm not *that* brave)
>Daisy when you're sixty-five?"
>"Do you remember what happened after tea?
>George Ernest walked into the sea."

Stuffed with creamed spinach
she danced largo,
watching a violin pluck a mot juste,
the musician balance his bow
against the full moon.
A Mediterranean haze from her hill
toughened the plywood houses to
hardness of the rock behind.
A streamlined avenue cut her land in two,

wheeled salesmen to their wives;
cheap lovers in expensive cars could show
she had lived wrong,
her dressed up company a joke,
her children useless as the words of an old song.

    Sitting at a long, low table
    I celebrate the High Mass of your love
    not in Latin: without music,
    formal as the sea.

AFTER THE REVOLUTION

The blood on the windows is fresh,
Most of the windows are broken.
Walls slough their cracks.
As the wounds close
My enemies
Tighten in my arms like burnt flesh.
A pair of trousers billows down the gutter
Making an obscene joke.
Far off, a wheel sighs
On the other side of the moon.
In the house across the street the empty rooms
Have murdered each other.
Water whispers through the drains
Into my hands.
I lean my sail, ready
To break records, move darkness into light;
Shove my arms in the barrel
For a treasure like snow, like the sea, the sun;
Come up salty, clutching a dead fish—
Its mouth open,
Its eyes pickled.
There's time to sleep before morning.
I roll back the stone from my tomb,
And let the dead day rise.

THE SCIENCE OF BUILDING

A beam so balanced needs no help:
The cantilever like the rods upon a clock.
Churches are built from it and great glass windows.

The mind in action thrusts
From the center of our weakness the force
To master rock,

Suspending the dark
At intervals as a word throws light
Or the shored sea sings.

When order is natural
The world rings
Like the body of a bell.

You and I under this roof
Watch the naked air between us
Grow solid at a touch.

IN DAVID'S STUDIO

Jean Harlow's nailed in the alcove,
Her belly bursting like the bloated
Flowers that don't make a garden
Five stories above the beach. Shall I jump?
If I land in water, I'll swim awhile.
But it's rock from here to there.
A black cat stands on white steps below us
Licking her whiskers. The hungry portrait of
Mr. Isherwood lies trapped
Between his bowl of fruit and withered books.
Who will write a prayer for Christopher
Or any of us hanging from these hooks?
Like Soutine and his slabs of meat
We stink in every sort of weather.
Goodnight, David, I'll dance the way you paint:
The snakes are singing round my feet.

DWIGHT   Dwight Robhs, who was born in 1940, lives in New
ROBHS   York City and works as a free-lance writer and editor. He
attended the School of General Studies at Columbia University.

SHADOW SONG

Here in this morning garden tensed with sun
in frosty, stark and perfect air bright lancings
and shakings of sunlight streak and spill the shadows
blunt, dark and complex where each object stays
or moves . . . the darkness of brightened things
half-lit like the faint west moon above
the shadow locked and sun-shocked hills . . .

The rosebush lifts above me to the day,
its shadows dent and rill and knot my seeing,
cut and darken the earth, reset this piece of world
minute by minute with tangles of blocked light . . .
as I do . . . shadows are real ask anyone
who's lived by telling time; substance defeats
my half-illumined certainties . . .

The roses sprung and lifted to the light
sway, palpable and amazing on the lithe
tangled, webbed, spiked stems; they gleam
and fill with richness, wound and unwound
in their darknesses . . . I let my mind fill now
above the dark of thought, like anyone
netted in a life of spikes, I sway
into the shadowless sun.

NOVEMBER, DUSK

The worn leaves wilt in the wearing rain
pittering, soft, steady, in this meagre grey atmosphere
everything that can die is dying . . .
your face is pale the water beads your hair

stirs it along the temples, your wool hat
smells dark and wet,
there's a wilt about us . . .
the watery air is an ache to breathe

I'm tired of walking and your hand
feels frailboned and light as a bird's wing . . .
I feel the leaves tear under us;
soaked and heavy others drop spinless

and *plut* on the earth like rags . . .
I think about that:
the way things fall . . .
a child's shirt is hung on a short bare treelet,

in this clearing, pale white and dripping
two short limbs thrust through the sleeves . . .
"It looks like a scarecrow," you say and then we're talking
brightly, briefly but we don't admit yet

that the walk isn't working . . .
our voices seem grey and we stop
at the end of the clearing
and put our hands in our pockets and look at the ground . . .

you see it first and point:
it looks like soggy leaves then isn't:
is a beaten flurry of feathers
long, clean white bones thin as a breath,

all that's left of what fell
greying away . . . there's no flesh, one feather
flickers slightly in the beading rain;
my finger traces where there was an eye . . .

things wear out and drop to earth
but the chemicals work and stir again

and it all returns in some way or other
in the gross crops of the earth . . .

suddenly I smile at you and want to laugh a little
because I'm thinking of lighter things than those . . .
that don't wear out . . . the lighter part of things
never falls . . . I hold you and say nothing . . .

in the lighter part of us both I hold you
and joy in the heft of your being
and feel the lift of you . . . unfalling, unfalling,
and wherever you look
you won't find the rotting feathers and bones of it . . .

TURN OF THE CENTURY BLUES
for Larry Cohen
(*from* Poems for the Future)

Some hundred steps from my door the dirt road joins
the paved, and streetlights start;
the still unblemished, crusty, snowy ice
(freezing rain has worn as slick and smooth
as other icy falls have worn my time)
makes each step a threat, skids
and teeters on each shift of ground
keep me to the brink of falling;

Overhead
the frost-hung wires ripple in the wind,
faintly clink and chime,
and gleam in manmade light between the earth
and sky of ice
where the unshaken stars flash heatlessly

And where (though one can't see them) spacecraft speed
soundless and remote, where messages
from poles and suns and men spill through the void.
With a letter to mail I balance down the road,
follow the frozen wires through the trees
dark in their snow and silence, reach route 1
where tires and human trackings mucked the snowfall,
tramped and slashed to ribbons and to slush.

(This too, in some faint way, was done to me)
The lights of Boston glitter in the east
heatless; a jet screams faintly, out of sight . . .
Below the hill somewhere a truck is groaning
and clanking its rhythmic chains; the heavy wires
flow and stagger east

With night talk and night terrors
across the snowbound country . . .
(And this I understand in my own nerves,
all the technology of love) I slog
through slush and mud with a firm, sloppy walk,
stop at the mailpost, scrape away the ice

and drop my mail into the frozen box,
and lean a moment looking into space
(fingers melting their blurred shape in the frost,
losing heat) lean and stare,
think of a dot of human warmth out there,
dream of the mail to Venus near the sun.

CRAZED BY EARTHLIGHT

The moon he meant was not the moon he found:
the cycles that spun and drew the tones from blood
and left it silver as his lady's hair;
and left them both eroded in their dream
in incidental moonlight merely true,
was not.

The lover (beyond his atmosphere
sealed in his warmth and light
into the spacious darkness as into
a wish
or deep into the mind of sleep
bound in logic that leaves waking strange)
probed:

And to his instruments a surface rose
abandoned to the universal cold;
and he left tracks across the desolation
under stars that never soften
where every day is night.

At the end of the myth
across a space one only guesses at
on a bare world that spins in death
on dull soil pitted like old flesh
this incidental, barren heaven
blinding in the factual sun
among eroded pinnacles
is not the moon at all.

TO AUTUMN

Countless sparrows riot in the trees,
The air stirs dryly and the landscape stiffens,
Thinned woods fill with shadow and I feel
The tears of another century rise
And stop—And I know why they wept
Or said they wept: it takes you as the wind
Unwinds a shape in the dark leaves, sparrows
Stutter in the sky . . .

You want to cry:
"These sensations dim and drum in me,
The bones of life now show beneath the skin
And shadows like the footfalls of centuries
Stalk through the woods and stalk across my lawn . . ."

You know it was all real: priapic
Shelley wasted with abstract love, and Keats
Ached his gleaming, shadowed head and saw
The mournful body of the season move
Like mist across the fields of all his days . . .

The sparrows wheel and gust through crinkly air
And scatter; darkness fills the woods in
As gleaming silence fills me—The fluent
Raptures of old grief are stuttered now . . .
You see the form of Autumn stir and stride
And tangle through the shadows with her scythe
And hear it sweep and whisper like the wind
That starts and gusts through the stunned leaves.

THE ASTROLOGER'S PROGRESS

for Alan Leo

He woke up in the iron mornings; cold
pressed at the windows, seeping through the boards;
the scythe of days rose glittering in the east
before his sun could rise.
His mother setting out the breakfast plates
moved like an ax and hummed a chilly psalm,
tilting her body like a haft to serve
coffee and eggs among dull pewter glints.
She wore the Devil thin, she always said,
her narrow head aimed always at her son.
Her hands cut downward when she spoke of God.

He shivered in the yard before his chores.
A pyramid of cordwood by the fence
between himself and any time to rest.
Not yet sunrise all his stars were out
glittering in degrees that urged and checked him.
He braced and raised the axhead to the sky,
feeling the heaven's vise and the slow grind
of turning earth that honed him to an edge.

Behind him in the house his mother slashed
at dishes, beds and streaks of dirt or dust
that gathered under doors or window cracks,
violent at gaunt work while outside
he marked the time to dawn with steady strokes,
and made a clock of labor. Overhead
the aspects wheeled, the oppositions tensed;
he split the dead wood never letting up
until the karmic chips lay all around
and like the past the logs were cut to kindling
ready for burning.

Each section of himself had felt the cuts.
Each time and thing he was had been cut down
and split to pieces.
Before the sun came up he made a hymn
of chopping and a sacrament of scythes:
whose destiny is flame must first be wood.

LITTLE EGYPT
for King Tut and Jon Briggs

Now on this inner wall
the harvests are being
laid up; the heavens have a human form,
gods and men mix with grave
responsible dignity.
Those priests at the edges, no doubt corrupt,
bless nevertheless; men
at prayer chafe for their beer
and the laborers groan and ache, no doubt.

That warlike Pharoah, lord
of light and dark, divine,
died shrivelled in politics, body
rotless like a long pressed
butterfly, fragile,
light as the dust: lust, greed, fear, boredom,
are shadows in the stone
rhetoric of grand poses;
each figure merely
what he was meant to be.

In solemn order and
inflexible harmony the men
remote as gods elegantly chiseled
show a single side not
rendered realistically,
fool no eye.
Each lord and slave has room enough
fitted in unyielding space just so
to maintain order in this dream of truth.

The tender sun that blesses eternal harvests,
as though time were a wall
where things can stay
as meant,
with graceful hands
with shadows in the hollows
fondly touches the poignant falsehoods
of men and gods who kept their places,
lights in its stone way
dreams carven for the dead;
casts unmoving shadows deep in stone.

PERSONNEL MAN IN A DESERTED CEMETERY
for Jon Beckmann

Like tombstones (standing in my consciousness
in a rickety graveyard by a vanished town
found while walking to bury last week's life
in Autumn country where the maples flame)
applications thrust into my attention
conceal who is behind them, styled to show
the lives inscribed and xeroxed had no gaps
or breakdowns, how they crossed from work to work
(as stoic and certain as I crossed the stream
from stone to slippery stone to reach the graves)
and never fell from grief or strayed to love . . .

In Autumn country where the ground grows hard
around imperfect resumes that list
credentials of the dead, unvarying,
narrow them down to only dates
and a line or two of stylized remorse . . .

In Autumn country where the leaves fall dead
alone in the anonymity
of monuments and forms a man fills out
(my personal files like tombstones in my head)
in wordless air I only heard the leaves
rattling down the way a life goes down
in wispy, papery sounds: I bury her,
and it, and him, and her, and her, and her.

LUNCH HOUR

Light plaited by ragged branches
binds our old lady professor to the lawn;
in the supernal heat of summer noon
she seems an entree for the ancient sun;
stretched flat her head supported by a book
a wispy woman in the greedy field,
white hair woven in the grass and weed.

Having browsed on tended knowledge all these years
she's tender and replete; domestic eyes
glaze now with understanding, dim the light;
she senses now the flower's cutting edge,
the dirge of insects and the knell of sky.
She understands, looks something like a lamb
with comic head pressed in a plate of greens,
foolish, unblinking, desperate eyes
reflect the rasping cutlery of time.

The whetted summer draws another breath,
plaited shadows truss her to the hour
as to a spit, the flowers gleam
the light of famished sun.

KAREN   *Karen Swenson, born in 1941, lives in Brooklyn. She*
SWENSON   *graduated from Barnard College, took her M.A. at*
New York University, and now teaches at New York's City College in
the SEEK and open enrollment programs. Her poetry has been extensively
published in literary and "slick" magazines.

WHY DIDN'T ANYONE TELL HESTER PRYNNE?

Pity him up to his waist in middle age,
neither celibate nor pervert in ceramics, only ultimate
with a finger caught in the clay cookie jar.

Leading her under the slatted moonlight
of palm trees, opening, shutting,
like a nervous venetian blind—
he said shyly,
"Have you ever done this before?"
She said, "No,"
curling her toes expectantly into the sand.
God sighed relief through his grey beard.

I don't know what happened to him. But she went home,
a smug pendulum of skirts, to inform her husband,
who had angelic nightmares ever after,
"Gabriel told me to."

DEAR ELIZABETH;

We are almost all homely,
beauty being rare as a round stone,
and I was once homelier than thou,
        pocked teeth, long nose, plain geometry jaw,
        an unleavened matso angling down the street,
        pigeon-toed strip of bespectacled lath.
The swan's story is a sweet one,
but it is a puff-ball beast.
Robins, April pretty, live on worms
to become unnoticeable by June.
        But the hatched hawk, gall-eyed
        in clumsy fluff between feet and beak,
        lives on fought flesh—waiting
        for shoulders to lean upon the wind.
I tell you this to keep comfort till your time.
A man is held stronger by beauty he knows
than any loveliness his eye can see.
        And don't mind Helen with Grecian ships,
        that is the male's most fervent legend,
        told by a wanderer totally blind.

HECUBA

Hecuba I want to know,
behind that mask
taut and intransigent as the glaze on my best china,
what grimace did you make
when Hector at Achilles' heel flopped like a fish
over the old dishcloth heaps of other dead men.

The flies
rose and settled
rose and settled
play parachutes disturbed by chariot wheels.

Did you think how luxuriant
the grass would be next year
rooting around Troy's wall?
Or of wars and whores and how
old men pimp the prostitute of death
to watch the young men lay her?

Some women wear their dead
as generals their medals,
a decoration of their own bravery.
They were able to bear this death.

Did you put a black handkerchief around his picture
and send the maid out
for the wax smugness of a lily?
More than two thousand years later,
two thousand years of the aphorism of graves and grass
(neither eggbeaters nor philosophy change anything)

I have a son,
a minnow in time's mouth. Hecuba,
behind old Homer's blind mask,
I want to know.

HOOKS AND EYES

Irish lace and linen—
she had the design right,
the skirt's mountain laurel pucker,
but no hooks and eyes.

So she sewed me in,
a last minute needle
through my first communion—
my marriage to Christ.

The next time it was grandma's
curdled wedding gown,
a supple splurge of satin.

Her damned needle basted me in again,
a lean noose loop—a turkey's zipper.
Through a succession of dresses
her loose stitch has pulled

pattern and fabric to the scissor's mouth.
Only now I realize
that's what she's always done;
gathered me into the paradigm, a slack abstract.

I bend my coffin cloth of flesh
basted hem to skin.
She's forgotten the hooks and eyes
again and sewed me in.

THE PRICE OF WOMEN

Every woman, you say, has her price:
a house with trees and tricycles,
a yellow porcelain sink that matches
shine to shine the kitchen cabinets,

and some are more expensive
requiring Tiffanys and other labels
draped over their luncheon chairs.

These are the bargains of love
or quiet or just another body to be by.

But are they? Isn't this the way we
counter what we will not give, a game
of poker chip exchange—an emerald for
emotion, not an equal sign

but the ellipse of instead of—
because what would I do if
you or anyone walked into the room

in the middle of the commercial
and asked for my life?

THE ECLIPSE

It was getting dark
as we walked across the park.
Children and adults
with pieces of cardboard
waited on the grass for the eclipse:

waited to center the sun,
pull it through a pinhole
threading it over their shoulder
onto a blank piece of paper—
a reaction of an action like a poem.

But we did not wait.
Too eager for each other
to care about heaven's chiaroscuro
we scattered our shoes
like Saturday afternoon beer cans

and while those outside
focused the concentric shadings—
circle of corona and circle of penumbra—
on the secondary cause of paper
so as not to go primarily blind

we, with the somber sky,
shadow on shadow, without
the security of secondary interventions,
while sun and moon coaxialed obscurity,
fell flesh to flesh into sightlessness.

A FAMILY

Voice muggy with affection and coffee cake
she keeps her sons arranged;
one against the bookcase,
the other at the piano,
with her smile darned like her nightgown;

while her husband on the wall
scuttles behind the pulp of his paintings.
Still cobwebbed by the lines of his last revolt

the sinews of his parents' care
support his Brooklyn Bridge—
little white tentacles, like mold
against a tomato sunset.

She licks her finger under the lamplight,
blots the crumbs up from the table.
She has always been satisfied.

That satisfaction wraps around them,
a bandage of all the lace her nightgown never had,
knotted to the torn sheets that cleaned the windows.

And when she rises
sucking the last crumb from her finger
to meet the challenge of their hunger again,
the nightgown swings, swings,
a pendulum on the back of the bathroom door.

JEAN   *Jean Valentine was born in Chicago in 1934. A graduate of*
VALENTINE   *Radcliffe College, she presently teaches in the*
English department at Hunter College. She has two collections of poetry
in print: Pilgrims, *published by Farrar, Straus & Giroux; and* Dream
Barker, *published by Yale University Press, which won the Yale Younger*
Poets award in 1965.

SOLOMON

Still, gold, open-handed,
sad King Solomon
listened: they started,
weightless, close to his car,
sweet as bees.

One with light breasts and knees
danced with herself before Solomon,
one stood by with barbarian eyes
mad for Solomon,
one, a child, even touched his face

and he smiled in his clothes,
shut his eyes.

Solomon sat by a white pond
his skin thin gold
and his head down.

One stood by with barbarian eyes
mad for Solomon.
She came to his hands,

light, far, anyone
or no one. Solomon
touched her eyes.

THE SUMMER HOUSE

I

She took his hand
so he brought her to his country:
'See it is dry': and

it was a light field, water,
a tree loud as water
in that wind.

—In your country
there is a light field, water.

Your body is in this wind,
I am in your mouth, your hand.

II

There were times
out of time's drag
we'd be without fixed faces
bodies or words; times

held like a feathery scene
on a Quimper plate: v's of quick birds
in their aviary sky, blue flowers
strung all around the dot-faced boy and girl:

all afternoon the sunlight ticked across
sleep, across our borrowed house.

III

The angels we made in the snow
are blown and the shapes at the snow's edge
are only themselves again

and we our taller selves
smoke between the house and the woods' edge,
dying to come in or have snow:

—Does he love her? She loves,
he loves, they

love the old stories of the snow
and the look of the house. Together so.

IN THE MUSEUM

There is a stone
where the Buddha was.
Nothing: air,

one footprint; his chair
a stone.
We stood

back, out of harm;
smiled; right?
went on.

The next room, love,
was funnier: all that love-making
in broad daylight,

and every one of them smiling.
Back where the Buddha was, the stone,
happy as God,

grinned like bone,
love: the air,
asking nothing,

smiled everywhere.

Come.

DOUGLAS WORTH   Douglas Worth, born in 1940, lives and teaches in Massachusetts. He grew up in Swarthmore, Pennsylvania, and Bangalore, India, and attended Swarthmore College and Columbia University. His poetry has appeared in many literary magazines.

STRAP HANGER

Half-curled above some lady's shoulder
the nails chipped
like the blades of old tools,
the skin indifferent, a hide
for all weathers

it bears a web of veins
delicate
as the skeleton of a boy's ship
still drying
in a vise.

MARRIED 2½ WEEKS

Only the half-perception
of new weight
words carry
between the two of us,
each thinking of the other now
as home

home still an infant
place of tenderness
the store-proud objects
settling in
each time we come across them
with our lives.

COCOONS AT THE WINDOW
for CBW

All winter, strung from nails, they knocked in wind
like ghostly fists of summer at the pane,
crusted for weeks with a thick glaze of snow
and buried in our minds a month ago.

Tonight, floating in darkness near the sill,
the silky wings, still tender with long sleep,
begin to stiffen, trembling, as when wind
glistens across the stretched skin of a sail.

BUCKEYE

sun-freckle
dancing
on summer's nose

bright pulse
on the slender
meadow-stalk.

MUSE

When you come carelessly
naked from the shower
passing from room to room
shaking out your hair

what can I do but follow

while something of that weight
and cast-off radiance flows
gathers and flows again
down the blank page.

METAMORPHOSES

Like a packed bud
rounding itself in the night,
its filaments poised
at thresholds of sun,

or a great cloud
of faintly-luminous dust
suddenly caving
inward to a star,

the known contours of self
give way
as darkness
goes molten.

BOURGOGNE

We saw too many Christs—his death became
part of the landscape, like the hanging-tree
pictured in every tenth-grade history—
a heritage, no one of us to blame.

Prague broke as we left Autun; Daley's men
butchered our stay in Paris, hounding us
till all that lifting harmony of glass
and stone at Sainte Chapelle had seemed undone.

Back in New York, *The Times* feels heavy, day
skids by on squealing rubber—as we'd feared
things were not changed by nights when stars appeared
so close our hands might have brushed them away,
or noons of sunlight where we lay and fed
each other's honied mouths with wine and bread.

THE RETURN

Then the Rhine Valley. March. April. Advancing
against the V-2's, while the cherry trees
spattered the hills like shrapnel, on our knees
we came to where bright water bugs were dancing.

For thirty days gauze and a string of tags
composed a hero's story—death undone,
my lips could find no meanings when the sun
crept like a Yellow Jacket down the rags
left for my scarecrow limbs . . .

   put out to drowse
long mornings on the valleyside, I grew
simple as leaves, resolving in the blue
each plane's drone to a murmuring of boughs—
home in my yard, a boy climbing with ease
to watch the high white blossoms crawl with bees.

INDEX OF AUTHORS AND TITLES

INDEX OF FIRST LINES OF POETRY